FOREIGN EXCHANGE CONCEPTS AND ARITHMETIC

EXPLAINED

Fundamentals of Forex Made Easy to Understand

Sugata Datta

notionpress.com

INDIA · SINGAPORE · MALAYSIA

The beautiful thing about learning is that nobody can take it away from you – B. B. King.

Contents

Foreword

I was very happy to learn that my colleague from Bank of India, Mr Sugata Datta, has written a book on Foreign Exchange. I could read the book rapidly and was delighted to see that the book explains terms of exchange in a simple and meaningful way.

Foreign exchange is central to international trade and global finance. In a world where goods, services, capital and ideas move across borders with increasing ease, the ability to understand foreign exchange is no longer the domain of specialists alone. Bankers, finance professionals, students, entrepreneurs and policy makers alike require a clear grasp of how currencies are priced, traded and managed.

Foreign exchange is often perceived as complex and intimidating. Technical terminology, market conventions and intricate calculations can create difficulties for learners. The true challenge is not merely to explain concepts, but to present them in a logical, practical and arithmetic-driven manner that bridges theory with real-world application.

This book, "*Foreign Exchange: Concepts and Arithmetic – Explained*", addresses that challenge with clarity and precision. It systematically builds the reader's understanding from foundational ideas to practical computation. Beginning with domestic and foreign currencies and the nature of foreign exchange markets, the book explains how currencies behave as commodities and how exchange rates are formed and quoted.

A distinguishing strength of this work is its emphasis on the arithmetic of foreign exchange. Topics such as merchant rate calculations, cross rates, forward margins, value dates and forward contracts are presented step-by-step, in a lucid manner. It helps to develop both conceptual clarity and computational confidence. Practical aspects such as early delivery, cancellation and extension of contracts further enhance the real-world relevance of the material.

By covering foreign currency accounts, types of exchange rates, and cross-currency forward rates, the book provides a comprehensive framework that covers market practices. The reader is not only introduced to the mechanics of foreign exchange, but also guided through the conventions and calculations that underpin everyday banking and treasury operations.

This work will serve as a valuable resource for students of banking and finance, professionals in foreign exchange and treasury functions, and anyone seeking a structured and practical understanding of currency markets. It succeeds in demystifying a subject that is essential to modern economic activity.

I am confident that this book will become a trusted companion for learners and practitioners who wish to master both the concepts and the arithmetic of foreign exchange.

Dilip G Patwardhan

Former Chief Executive

Foreign Exchange Dealers' Association of India

(FEDAI)

Preface

I have found that in banks, there often exists a certain aura surrounding personnel who handle foreign exchange business. Forex Officers are frequently regarded with a sense of curiosity and envy, sometimes even admiration, as colleagues wonder about the nature and complexity of their work.

Questions naturally arise: what risks arise from fluctuations in exchange rates if a decision on a transaction is delayed? What determines buying and selling rates, forward premia and discounts, and the entire spectrum of exchange rate quotations? Some understanding develops when banking staff prepare for professional courses.

Nevertheless, significant conceptual gaps often remain.

The field of Foreign Exchange covers multiple functional areas, including exchange rate calculations, remittances, trade finance, and non-resident deposits. While all these areas are important, the **mechanics of exchange rates** require a particularly clear conceptual understanding.

This book aims to address that need by explaining the **underlying rationale behind exchange rate calculations**. In the modern banking environment, which is heavily dependent on computerised systems, the calculation of rates has largely become a process of retrieving system-generated outputs. As a result, many practitioners are familiar with the final numbers but not necessarily with the logic or methodology used to derive them.

The purpose of this book is, therefore, to explain exchange rate mechanisms in a clear and structured manner - *particularly for readers who may not have prior exposure to the subject.* It would also be useful for professional users of foreign exchange, including exporters and importers as their businesses are heavily dependent on exchange rates.

During my own endeavours to deepen my knowledge of Foreign Exchange, I found that while there was an abundance of literature on trade finance, and numerous regulatory guidelines covering areas such as remittances and deposits, there was relatively little material dedicated specifically to the **concepts and operating mechanics of exchange rates**. Where exchange rates were discussed, the treatment was generally brief, covering a few chapters or at most, one section of the book. Moreover, although illustrative examples were provided, the underlying reasoning behind the calculations—*the "whys"*—was rarely explored in sufficient depth.

The gap in the available literature became my principal motivation for writing this book, drawing upon several decades of professional experience in the foreign exchange and international banking domain.

A practical issue in writing a book about exchange rates is the challenge posed by continuously changing currency values. When the idea of this book was first conceived, the exchange rate of USD against INR was in the 70's. By the time I started writing, the rate had moved into the 80's, and now it is well into the 90's.

Given this dynamic environment, preparing consistent numerical illustrations can be difficult. Accordingly, for the purpose of examples and calculations in this book, the USD-INR rate has been assumed to be in the upper 80's / lower 90's range.

The intention is not to predict any prevailing market levels, but to focus on the principles and methodologies *which remain constant irrespective of exchange rate movements.* These principles remain equally relevant in a fully computerised environment and in the evolving landscape shaped by Artificial Intelligence.

I hope that readers—particularly banking professionals, students of international finance and others interested in foreign exchange, including exporters and importers—will find the book engaging and useful in developing a clearer understanding of exchange rate mechanisms.

I place on record my deep gratitude to Mr. R. Govindarajan, my longstanding colleague and friend – and a forex expert in his own right, for painstakingly reviewing the manuscript and providing numerous useful suggestions.

My thanks also go out to Mr. Hrishikesh Bukate, a top-class creative artist and budding entrepreneur, for his efforts in designing the appealing cover of the book.

Writing the book has been an immensely satisfying experience, and I hope readers will enjoy it as much as I have enjoyed writing it.

Any suggestions or ideas for improving the book will be welcome and I can be contacted at skdatta7777@gmail.com.

– SUGATA DATTA

Chapter 1

Introduction

The spirit of this introductory chapter will be appreciated, if it read in conjunction with the Preface, as the Preface spells out the objective of this book.

The book seeks to cater to those initiated - as also those uninitiated - to the world of foreign exchange. Effort has, therefore, been taken to build up a gradual take-off slope on which even the uninitiated can hop on comfortably. Thereafter, as the book progresses, it reveals the world of greater complications and diverse concepts in foreign exchange, which it is hoped will be very useful for even those who have worked in the forex areas for many years.

The goal of this book is to *explain*. Explain the very basics of foreign exchange and *explain* why the calculation of forex rates happen the way they do. It is as if to lift a curtain and peek inside to see - and understand - the underlying mechanics.

Therefore, throughout the book, an effort has been made to illustrate the concepts with flow diagrams and provide relevant examples and exercises. This foundation of knowledge is reinforced by providing exercises, many of them related to examples from the real world and, thereafter, systematically solving the exercises using logical steps.

The common thread throughout the book is, therefore, to make the Reader *understand* what is being discussed.

The book, after covering basic features of currencies, foreign currencies and foreign exchange markets, introduces the concept of regarding any foreign currency as a commodity (ie., something that can bought and sold), rather than money.

Two chapters deal with cross rates and it is explained why, whereas in some cases, cross rates are arrived at by multiplication, in other cases, they derived by division – and that too after interchanging the bid and offer rates. Although it may be easy to remember formulae for such calculations, once the mechanics are understood, the concepts become crystal clear.

While the book covers other related topics like different types of accounts and various types of value dates, efforts have been taken to provide the rationale behind the calculation of different types of rates, like TT Buying, TT Selling, Bill Buying and Bill Selling rates.

These should be of interest, not just to bankers and students of international finance, but also to exporters and importers. While interbank rates can be obtained from one of the many sources in public domain, this community will benefit by understanding how their bankers work out the rates and apply them, thereafter, in international trade transactions.

A sizeable portion of the book has been reserved for forward contracts and different scenarios that can arise after a forward contract is booked – like early delivery, cancellation and extension.

Here again, effort has been taken to unveil the mechanics of how charges for each of these variants are calculated. This, it is felt, would also be of interest and value to exporters and importers, since forward contract is the most commonly used derivative instrument in international trade and it is in the interest of such business entities to understand the *why's* of the transactions and the *how's* of the calculations.

Chapter 2

Domestic and Foreign Currencies

2.1 WHAT IS A CURRENCY?

Money / Domestic Currency / National Currency / Foreign Currency

To begin our understanding what foreign exchange is, it is necessary to understand what a currency is. And also, what a foreign currency is.

When we talk of currency, we generally mean domestic currency or what, in simple language, called money. So, what is money?

Money is a medium of exchange. It can be used for exchange into goods and services. A ₹ 100- currency note can be used to exchange for (ie., buying) goods and services whose value is ₹ 100-. That means, it is a store of value.

This would, however, not be true if the seller of the goods (when we say goods, we mean services also) does not accept the ₹ 100 currency note.

Hence, two characteristics of money are that:

1. It should be store of value

2. It should be acceptable to everyone.

We have recently seen the importance of acceptability as a characteristic of money, when the ₹ 500 and ₹ 1,000 denomination currency notes were demonetised on 8th November 2016. With once stroke of action, these notes ceased to be acceptable by everyone and, hence, they ceased to be money.

And, as stated earlier, domestic currency is the same as money for that country. Hence Indian Rupees is the domestic currency for India and is, hence, money in India.

Domestic currency can also be called national currency, because most countries have their own currencies, eg., Indian Rupees in India, Japanese Yen in Japan, Thai Baht in Thailand and Mexican Pesos in Mexico.

However, there are some countries which use a common currency which cannot be called belonging to one particular country. An example of this is the Euro (EUR) which is the domestic currency for some of the countries of the European Union like France, Germany, Spain, Italy and Belgium. Such countries do not have a national currency and, instead, their money is a common currency of the European Union.

And interestingly, while US Dollar (USD) is the domestic and national currency of United States of America (USA), the USD has also been adopted as the domestic currency by a number of other countries like Ecuador, El Salvador, Zimbabwe, Panama and a few more countries. Such countries, therefore, also do not have any unique national currency of their own.

Having understood what domestic currency (or money) is, let us now understand what a foreign currency is.

Foreign currency is a relative term. For residents of Singapore, Singapore Dollar is the domestic currency and constitutes money there. However, the same currency for an Indian in India, is a foreign currency. Singapore Dollar, in India, does not exhibit the two characteristics which are pre-requisites of money. It cannot be used as a medium of exchange in India. For example, suppose you took an autorickshaw from your house in Delhi to New Delhi Railway Station. Can you pay the rickshaw driver in Singapore Dollars? No, that would not be possible, as the rickshaw driver would not accept it as value for services rendered by him.

Hence, a foreign currency is the domestic currency (or money) of another country.

2.2 WHAT IS FOREIGN EXCHANGE?

Foreign exchange is the process of converting one currency into another currency. It is not necessary that one of the currencies is the domestic currency. The conversion can be between two currencies, both of which are foreign currencies. Hence, while converting INR into USD constitutes foreign exchange, converting, say, EUR or GBP into USD also constitutes foreign exchange.

When foreign currencies are exchanged, the value of the two currencies is not equal. This leads to the concept of exchange rates. Just like one pineapple is available for, say, INR 100-, in a similar way, one USD is available for, say INR 90. The exchange rate for USD, in this example, is therefore 90. In the same manner, there will be exchange rate for various other currencies against the INR, as also exchange rates for various currencies against each other. For example, one EUR is equal to, say, 1.20 USD, and so on.

2.3 WHY DO WE NEED FOREIGN CURRENCIES?

We need foreign currencies because it is not possible to obtain / manufacture everything that we need from domestic resources only. Take, for example, a large commercial airplane. India does not manufacture these and, hence, it has necessarily to buy them from foreign suppliers like Airbus and Boeing. And even if India was able to manufacture such airplanes, it may not have been able to produce them cheaper than what Airbus or Boeing can. That is because Airbus and Boeing have developed specialisation and expertise in manufacture of large airplanes through decades of experience and research. Therefore, in any case, we in India would need to buy the airplanes from abroad, say from Boeing.

Boeing is an American Company that is located in Seattle, USA. If we had to buy a Boeing airplane, we would have to pay them in their currency, that is in USD. We cannot pay them in INR because for Boeing, INR is a foreign currency and cannot be used a medium for exchanging into goods and services in USA. Hence, we would need to convert INR into USD and then pay the USD to Boeing.

The above example explains why foreign currency is required and why it is needed to exchange from one currency to another currency. The situation would be similar for any transaction which involved international trade, that is, where the buyers and sellers are from different countries. The need for foreign currency, thus, arises from the phenomenon of international trade.

Exercise 2

1. US Dollars is money in which of the following countries?

   a. USA

   b. Ecuador

   c. Panama

2. Which of the following is / are characteristic(s) of domestic currency?

   a. It should be a store of value

   b. It should be freely acceptable

   c. It should be exchangeable into a foreign currency

3. Which of the following statement(s) is / are true?

   a. All domestic currencies can be converted into foreign currencies

   b. In foreign exchange, one of the two currencies has to be a domestic currency

   c. Foreign exchange denotes conversion of one foreign currency into another foreign currency, only

4. If an Indian company in Mumbai required to buy machinery from Germany, it would have to pay the German supplier in which of the following?

   a. Indian Rupees

   b. Euros

   c. Either Indian Rupees or Euros

5. Mani Exports had exported 250 kgs of a generic pharmaceutical to an American company located in California. The exporter would require the export proceeds to be made available to it in which of the following currencies?

   a. Indian Rupees

   b. US Dollars

   c. Either Indian rupees or in US Dollars

Chapter 3

Foreign Exchange Rates

3.1 WHAT ARE FOREIGN EXCHANGE RATES?

Exchange Rates against Indian Rupees

Foreign exchange rates (or exchange rates) are the factors by which one currency can be expressed in terms of another currency. It is basically the price of a currency. What is the price of an apple? Rs 25. What is the price of a US Dollar? Rs 90. Expressed technically, 1 USD = INR 90, or USD INR rate is 90.

Cross Currency Exchange Rates

As against what has been explained above, foreign exchange rates often are quoted as the price of one foreign currency in terms of another foreign currency.

One water melon = INR 75.

One water melon = 125 grapes.

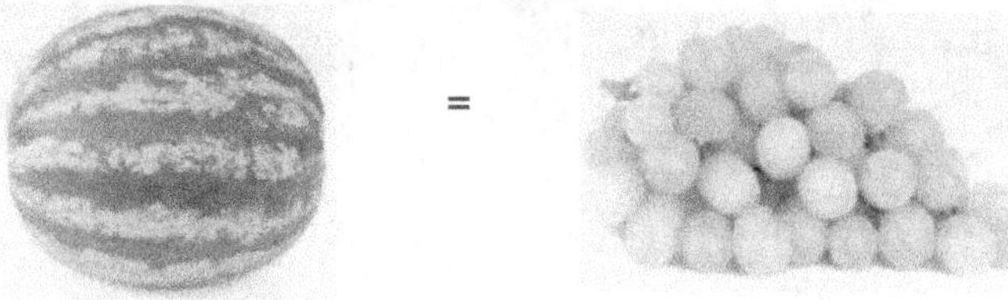

Figure 3.1 Cross rates for fruits

In the second statement, above, you will see that on both sides there are fruits. No Rupees.

Similarly, one US Dollar = 155 Japanese Yen, or USD JPY = 155.

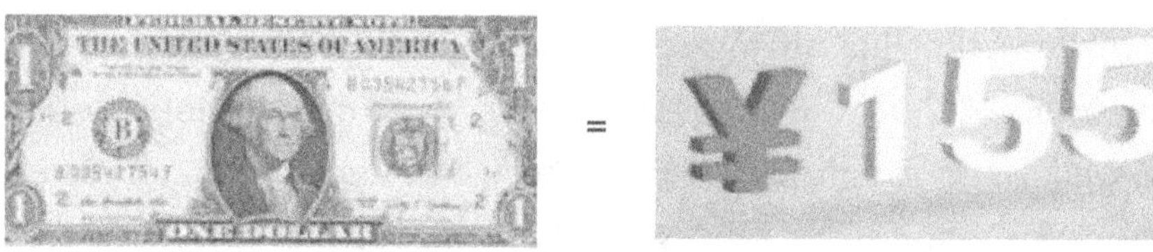

Figure 3.2 Cross rates for currencies

Here also, on both sides there are foreign currencies.

Foreign exchange rates change very frequently, often once in every 3 seconds. Hence the USD rate can move from 90.10 to 90.12 to 90.10 to 90.09 to 90.06 all within a space of 15 seconds!

3.2 WHAT ARE THE FACTORS THAT INFLUENCE FOREIGN EXCHANGE RATES?

Why do foreign exchange rates change so frequently? What are the factors that cause exchange rates to fluctuate?

Some of the factors are as follows:

- Economic Growth
- Fiscal Deficit
- Inflation

- Changes in Interest Rate
- Monetary Policy
- Balance Of Payments
- Central Bank Intervention
- Geo-Political Scenario
- Speculation

Let us now examine each of these factors.

3.2.1 Economic Growth

A country that has strong economic growth will be attractive for investments. Such investments could be from domestic sources as well as through external sources. Every investor looks for appreciation in his / her investment and a country exhibiting strong economic growth, would, naturally be an attractive destination from the point of view of attractive investment returns.

Hence foreign exchange will flow in. Let us say that US Dollars flow in. With excess supply of USD in the economy, the price of USD will automatically start to fall. Hence USD INR may move from 91.00 to 90.90 to 90.77 to 90.60 over a period of time. What does this mean? It means that the USD is becoming cheaper (depreciating) with respect to the INR, or that INR is appreciating in comparison to USD.

- Hence, strong economic growth = appreciation of the INR (home currency).

Figure 3.3 Relationship between economic growth and exchange rates

(The term "home currency" is also used since INR would be case only if we speak of India. In other countries, the "home currency" would be different. For example, JPY in Japan)

3.2.2 Fiscal Deficit

Readers would be aware that the Finance Minister of India, presents the Union Budget to the Parliament on the 1st February every year. The Budget is for the next financial year and it details the various sources and amounts of income that the Government expects to receive and the amounts of expenditure, under various heads, that the Government expects to incur. If the projected expenditure exceeds the projected income, there will be a shortfall (or deficit) and this is called the fiscal deficit. Fiscal deficits are normal, and in fact an indication of a healthy economy – so long as the fiscal deficit is manageable and kept under control. At present, the Government targets to keep the fiscal deficit at below 4.5%. (During the COVID years, the fiscal deficit was in excess of 9%).

A fiscal deficit can affect exchange rate depending on what type of measures the Government takes to plug the deficit. If it prints more currency (INR), the supply of INR will increase. The excess availability of INR will decrease its value, compared to other currencies. Hence the INR would depreciate.

If the Government chooses to plug the deficit by borrowing from abroad, the demand for foreign currencies will increase, which would increase their prices. Under this route also, therefore, the INR will depreciate since the foreign currencies will appreciate.

- Hence, increased fiscal deficit = depreciation of INR (home currency)

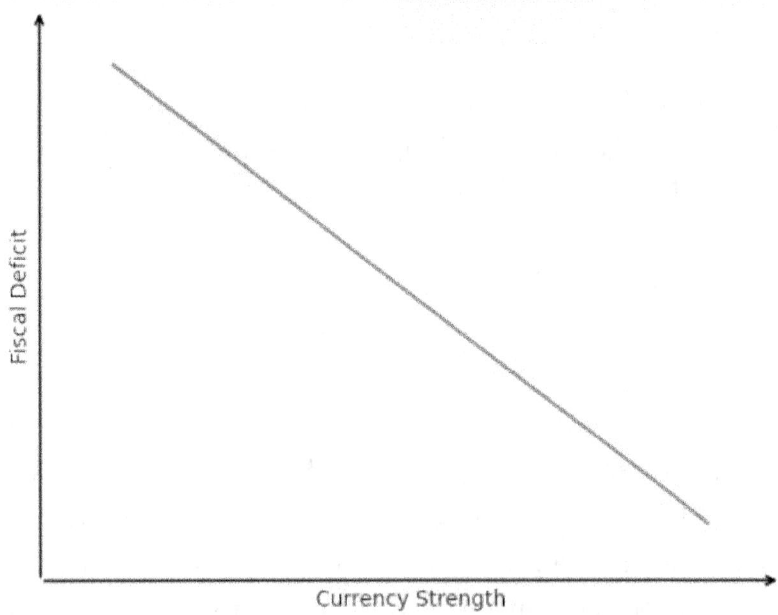

Figure 3.4 Relationship between fiscal deficit and exchange rates

(The reverse will be true for reduced fiscal deficit)

3.2.3 Inflation

The effect that inflation in a country has on the exchange rate is an extension of the concept of fiscal deficit. The Government may try to plug the deficit by increasing the supply of INR. One of the side effects of the increased supply of INR is that a situation is created where more money starts chasing the same amount of goods produced. Hence, the demand for goods increases (as everyone has more money) and this leads to increased price of goods, which is the same as inflation.

- Hence, increased fiscal deficit → increased inflation → depreciation of INR (home currency).

  (The reverse will be true for reduced inflation)

3.2.4 Changes in Interest Rates

You have just read that fiscal deficit leads to inflation. Inflation is not good, as it makes everyone poorer. For example, earlier if apples cost Rs 200- per kilo, it may now cost Rs 300- per kilo. You would have to pay additional Rs 100- to buy the same quantity of apples.

In order to keep inflation under control, therefore, the authorities would try and reduce the supply of money available with the public. How would they restrict the supply of money? By raising the price of money itself. That is, by raising interest rates.

As can therefore be observed, all these parameters are inter-related and ultimately affect the exchange rate in the same manner.

- Hence, increased fiscal deficit → increased inflation → rise in interest rates → depreciation of INR (home currency).

  (The reverse will be true for fall in interest rate)

3.2.5 Monetary Policy

Monetary Policy is a set of actions that are required to be taken in order to control the country's overall money supply with the objective of achieving the targeted level of economic growth.

Monetary policy setting is the responsibility of the central bank, ie., Reserve Bank of India, in our country. At present, RBI targets at keeping the inflation at a level of 4%, with an upper limit of 6% and a lower limit of 2%. One of the main tools available to RBI, under Monetary Policy, to keep inflation under check, is by adjusting interest rates. Hence, if the RBI is of the view that the economy has inflationary trend (over-heating) it will take a contractionary stand and raise interest rates. However, if the RBI is of the view that the economy needs a boost and more money needs to be put in the hands of the public, it will take an expansionary stand and reduce interest rates.

The effect that interest rates have on exchange rates has already been discussed in the preceding section.

3.2.6 Balance of Payments

The balance of payments for any country constitutes the net position of all its international payments and receipts. These include items on account of trade (for example, exports and imports) as well as items of services (for example, receipt of remittances from Indian workers from abroad, interest payments made on foreign borrowings). If the total amount of payments exceeds the total amount of receipts, the balance of payments will be negative. If the inverse is true, that is, if the total amount of receipts exceeds the total amount of payments, the balance of payments will be positive.

When the balance of payments is adverse, there will be demand for foreign currency as the receipts are not sufficient to cover the payments. This increase in demand would lead to increase in price of foreign currency, which would appreciate against the home currency (in India, INR).

In case the balance of payments is positive, there would be a surplus in supply of foreign currency, which would lead to a decrease in its price, causing the foreign currency to depreciate against the home currency.

- Hence, adverse balance of payment = depreciation of INR (home currency)

  (The reverse will be true if the balance of payments is positive)

3.2.7 Central Bank Intervention

As you have read earlier, the central bank is responsible for formulating the Monetary Policy. This includes trying to see that the exchange rate of the domestic currency, eg., INR, does not move to undesirable levels.

Here we have to be clear that no central bank can control the exchange rate of its domestic currency as the global foreign exchange market is just too large for any central bank to try and control it. Hence, for example, the RBI cannot announce that it will not allow the USD INR rate to fall beyond 90.50. If other economic factors as have been just discussed are exercising pressure on the INR, the INR is bound to depreciate to whatever level the economic forces permit it to, at that point of time. However, the stated policy of central banks is that, while they do not indicate any targeted level for the domestic currency, they do not like to have volatility in the market.

Volatility occurs when there are large swings in the exchange rates over a short period of time, say during the day. For example, the USD INR may swing from 89.90 to 90.00 to 90.85 to 90.50

to 90.75 to 91.00 to 90.20 to 89.90, all during the course of one day – a swing of 110 paise. Volatility can be caused due to sudden economic events, say declaration of a war somewhere, a violent geographical event like a tsunami, etc., or even due to speculations like which party will win the next elections, and so on.

The reason why central banks do not like volatility is because the quick changes in the exchange rates can harm and cause losses to genuine customers like importers, exporters and those making or receiving essential remittances like remittance of college fees, medical expenses, maintenance expenses, etc.

Central banks can reduce volatility by selling foreign currency (from their foreign exchange reserves) if the domestic currency depreciates suddenly and buying foreign currency if the domestic currency appreciates suddenly, thereby smoothening out the movements and bring a semblance of stability to the market. This is called central bank intervention.

This, however, cannot go on for ever, since the central bank would not have enough reserves to continually pump in or suck out foreign currency from the foreign exchange market, and that can be done in short bursts only. In either case, the exchange rate would be affected by the nature and amount of central bank interventions.

3.2.8 Geo-political Scenarios

The world is a very large place with over 225 countries and territories. The different countries have differing customs, ideologies and different levels of economic strength. While some countries are well developed, some others are developing and there are also countries that are categorised as Least Developed Countries (LDCs). Given the ideologies of different countries, there can be instances of tensions between two or more of them or there can easing of earlier tensions. For example, the war in Ukraine or the attack on Iran. At the same time, there are countries that may try to ease tensions and global cooperation – like the efforts taken by India at the G-20 Summit in 2023.

If tension erupts in the world, normal life and trade can be threatened. Investors immediately move towards less risky assets like gold, or a well-accepted currency like US Dollar. During such times, therefore, the USD will tend to strengthen (or appreciate) against most other currencies as demand for it increases. There will be spells of extreme volatility, as well.

- Hence, geo-political instability tends to lead to appreciation of USD. Which translates into weakening of INR against the USD.

(In case of easing of tensions, the safety status of USD decreases, thereby making it depreciate [in fact, to normalise] with apparent strengthening of other currencies, including INR).

3.2.9 Speculation

Speculation is the process of taking a view on a matter, without complete information on it. It is more by way of a hunch or "sixth sense". If I feel that in the upcoming US Presidential Elections, Mr X will win and that he is a strong leader, the USD will get a boost and strengthen against other currencies, I am speculating on the strengthening of the USD at a future date. It may turn out to be true or it may not turn out to be true. Mr X may lose the Election and even if he wins, the USD may not strengthen.

However, based on my view and a "feeling" that the USD will strengthen, I can proceed to buy USD against other currencies.

If many speculators think in the same way, there will be a buying pressure on the USD and it will strengthen just because of the that sentiment, much before the US Elections are actually held.

If the reverse hunch is true, then I can speculate on a weakening of the USD, and such speculative pressure could drive the USD down.

- Hence, exchange rates can be affected by speculation.

EXERCISE 3

1. Which of the following can influence exchange rates?

   Inflation

   Geo-political instability

   Reduction in interest rates

2. If a war-like situation arises in South East Asia, which of the following can be expected to happen?

   Appreciation of USD

   Increase in price of gold

   Appreciation in INR

3. Which of the following would have a weakening pressure on the INR?

   Increase in repo rate by RBI

   Surplus in balance of payments

   Weak economic data received from USA

4. An increasing fiscal deficit can be expected to lead to which of the following?

   Strengthening of INR

   Weakening of INR

   No effect on INR

5. When a central bank buys or sells foreign currency in the forex market in order to reduce volatility, what is that operation known as?

   Influencing

   Intervention

   Influx

6. There was a major volcanic explosion in Iceland which threw large amounts of ash high in the atmosphere. This disrupted Trans-Atlantic flights severely, consequent to which all flights between Europe and USA were grounded for a week.

   Which of the following would be expected to happen in such a situation?

   INR will weaken

   USD will weaken

   There will be no impact on the strength of the INR

Chapter 4

Characteristics of the Forex Market

4.1 WHAT IS A MARKET?

A market is a place where many buyers and sellers come together to buy or sell goods and services. The items being bought or sold could be fruits or vegetables or, even, foreign currencies. Buyers and sellers get together and determine, amongst themselves, a price at which the items can be exchanged. When we talk about foreign currencies being bought and sold, this price is nothing but what is called the exchange rate.

A market can be physical or it can be virtual. Most traditional markets, like say, vegetable markets, are physical where the buyers and sellers are present physically to buy and sell. (In fact, with today's e-commerce, even vegetable markets can be virtual, say, if you are ordering vegetables on line).

However, in foreign currencies, the markets are not physical and the transactions (buying and selling) are done on phone or through computer screens. There can be few cases of physical market place for foreign currencies also, for example, when you encash, say, US Dollar currency notes, at the counters of a bank or a money changer.

Figure 4.1 Forex Markets – Virtual and Physical

4.2 FOREX MARKET CHARACTERISTICS

Characteristics of the forex market are as follows:

4.2.1 Wide Participation

The foreign exchange is very large and global. The first major forex market that opens in the morning is the Sydney market and the last market that opens is the New York market. The market operates 24 hours on all weekdays and is closed on weekends. The world is divided into four forex zones, namely, Sydney, Tokyo, London and New York.

The total daily forex transactions is about USD 9.6 trillion – up from USD 7.5 trillion in 2022. Compare this with the daily transactions of USD 479 billion of Nasdaq, which is the largest stock exchange in the world and one would get an idea of the enormity of the forex market.

Some interesting facts about the forex market are provided here.

Over 170 currencies are exchanged in the market and the US Dollar is involved in 88% of the trades, the other major currencies being EUR (31%), JPY (17%) and GBP (13%).

[Note: You will find that the percentage of these four major currencies exceeds 100% and that is because currencies are always traded in pairs, and hence the percentages should be halved in order to be reckoned on a base of 100%.]

The maximum number of foreign exchange transactions take place from UK, USA, Hongkong, Singapore and Japan and these 5 centres account for 78% of the trades. Of these, UK is the dominant centre with 38% of the transactions being handled from there.

The maximum number of transactions took place in the EUR USD pair (22%), followed by USD JPY (13.5%) and GBP USD (9.5%).

Turnover in INR related transactions accounted for 1.6% of the daily global turnover and India, as a centre, accounted for 0.5% of the total turnover.

4.2.2 Free Floating Rates

Prices at which foreign currencies are exchanged are not regulated by any authority (barring some instances where central banks intervene) and the buyers and sellers are free to arrive at the price at which they are prepared to carry out the transaction. As a result, the rates are floating (not fixed) and foreign exchange rates change constantly—often by the second—during active trading hours in the global forex market

You have already read, in the last Chapter, about the different factors that have effect on foreign exchange rates. Consequently, forex rates are heavily affected by macro-factors and these increase the uncertainty and volatility of the forex market.

4.2.3 Global Influence

Forex markets are not only affected by their domestic economies; they are also affected by what happens globally. A volcanic eruption in Iceland that spews ash in the atmosphere and threatens flights between USA and Europe can induce a global shock followed by a flight towards safe assets and strengthening of gold and USD.

Similarly, if North Korea launches a test missile that falls in the nearby Sea of Japan, exchange rates of apparently unrelated currencies can be affected. A severe earthquake in Japan can, likewise, create shivers in the global forex market.

4.2.4 Competitive

The forex market is very large with USD 9.6 trillion daily transactions and the number of forex traders is estimated to be over 10 million. With such a large market and so many players, prices have to be competitive. Any trader quoting outside the ruling price range will automatically be ignored and the effective price will, at all times, be dictated by the forces of demand and supply.

Accordingly, it is also extremely difficult to manipulate the prices as the market is just too large. It would be as ineffective as drawing out a few buckets of water from an ocean. Such high levels of competition would automatically remove any uncompetitive player out from the market.

4.2.5 Risky

The fact that the exchange rates change very frequently makes the forex market a risky place to do business in.

Figure 4.2 Fluctuations in the forex market

A trader who bought USD INR at 92.00 can immediately incur a loss if, in the next moment, the rate changes to 91.99. Similarly, a trader who sold USD INR at 91.44 will immediately incur a loss if the rate changes to 91.45.

The amount may look small as the rate movement is only 1 paisa. However, if the deal (transaction) is for USD 1 million (which is quite a common deal size), the loss would be INR 10,000.

And if the transaction was for USD 10 million, the immediate loss would be Rs 1 lakh.

4.2.6 Acutely Information Sensitive

Foreign exchange rates can be acutely affected by announcements made with regard to various types of economic data. One typical example if the announcement of Non-Farm Payroll (NFP) data in USA. This data is released by the US Government on the first Friday of every month at 8.30 am New York time. It is an important economic indicator related to the unemployment position in the US.

Based on whether the actual numbers announced are better or worse than the expected numbers, acute volatility can be witnessed in the forex market, especially in relation to the EUR USD and GBP USD pairs.

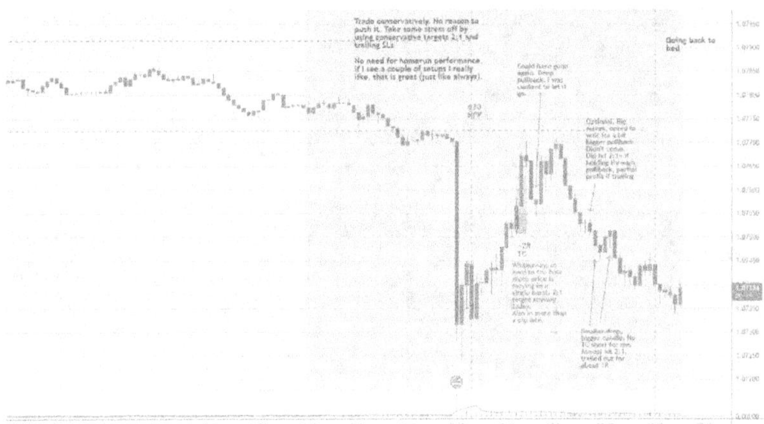

Figure 4.3 Volatility in EUR USD market following announcement of Non-Farm Payroll Data

The graph above is for EUR USD rates on 6th December, 2023. The NFP was announced at 6.30 am Mountain Time (USA), which is 8.30 am New York time, and that is a little after where the green shaded of the graph starts.

It will be seen that whereas the market was very quiet till then and the EUR USD movement was almost flat, no sooner than when the NFP data was announced, there was high volatility with rapid and large variations in the exchange rate (see inside the red circle).

Similar volatility can be witnessed often when important economic data is announced by Governments and central banks, although the extent of volatility would depend upon how important that information is at a global level.

Sometimes, speeches by Governors of leading central banks can also move exchange rates significantly as has been the case of movement in USD JPY following important announcements made by the Governor of Bank of Japan (which the central bank of Japan).

4.2.7 Central Bank Influenced

The effect of interventions by some of the important central banks in the world, like the Federal Reserve, European Central Bank (ECB), Bank of England, Bank of Japan, etc also can affect the foreign exchange market.

In India, similar moves by the RBI can influence the USD INR rates, and through that, the exchange rate of INR with other currencies like EUR, GBP, JPY, etc.

4.3 WHO ARE THE PARTICIPANTS IN THE FOREX MARKET?

4.3.1 Corporates

Foreign exchange is primarily required for conduct of international trade and these are handled by corporates who are exporters and importer. Corporates are, therefore, large participants in the forex market. Corporations can be private sector or public sector.

4.3.2 Individuals

Individuals also have need for foreign exchange. This could be on account of having to transfer money overseas, say towards gifts or education expenses or medical costs, etc. They could also be for maintaining foreign currency deposits in overseas banks.

4.3.3 Commercial Banks

Commercial banks are, probably, the biggest participants in the forex market. They predominantly enter the forex markets on behalf of their customers and this will be discussed in greater detail while studying buying and selling foreign currencies. Commercial banks also enter the forex market, on their own accord, by taking up proprietary trading positions.

4.3.4 Governments

Governments are also large players in the forex market. They may enter for raising loans and bonds or for repayment of their borrowings and interest payments. Governments also enter in order to park their surplus foreign exchange funds through deposits or global investments. Whilst, at times, governments can enter the forex market through the central bank, at other times, they enter the forex markets directly.

4.3.5 Forex Brokers

The role of brokers is to facilitate transactions by matching banks that want to buy forex with banks that want to sell forex. Interbank deals constitute approximately 46% of all deals and many of these are brokered deals – either through voice brokers or electronic broker platforms. While electronic trading dominates, voice brokers still account for a portion of the market.

Electronic broker platforms are also used by corporates, although mainly for the purpose of viewing exchange rates, rather than actually transacting by using them.

4.3.6 Central Banks

As has been brought out earlier, central banks have an important role to play in the forex market. While their participation is on much fewer occasions when compared to commercial banks, their transactions are significantly larger in size.

Hence, the presence, or lack of presence, of central banks can have important impact on the forex market.

4.3.7 Hedgers

Hedging, in foreign exchange, means to protect oneself from forex risks. Hence, a corporate, individual, or even a commercial bank, with an existing or anticipated foreign exchange asset / liability can participate in the forex market in order to use available products that serve to reduce the foreign exchange risk. These products include forward contracts, forex options and swaps.

For example, a corporate that has raised an External Commercial Borrowing (ECB) in USD, but has its revenues in Rupees may choose to cover its forex risk by using a hedging product like as US Dollar – Indian Rupee swap.

Similarly, an individual who has a deposit in a foreign country may hedge his / her foreign exchange risk by using a product like a forward contract or a currency option.

4.3.8 Speculators

Speculators enter the forex market solely for the opportunity to make a profit from the market. They do not have any genuine underlying transaction like an export receivable or an import payable, but they buy and sell currencies only for betting on the future trend so as to try and make a profit.

4.3.9 Arbitrageurs

Arbitrageurs fall in the category of speculators, who however, hedge their forex positions by eliminating the exchange rate risk completely. They simultaneously buy and sell foreign currencies and make a profit in the bargain.

The opportunity for arbitrage can arise for very short periods of time due to the global nature of the market and multiple time zones, coupled with imperfections in communication and information systems. Such situations can result in slight and temporary differences in the exchange rates in different forex markets, at the same time of the day.

Hence, if the EUR USD is quoted at 1.2020 in Bahrain and 1.2025 – at the same time in London, an alert forex trader can buy EUR at 1.2020 in Bahrain and simultaneously sell the same amount of EUR at 1.2025 in London, thereby earning a profit of USD 0.0005 for every Euro sold. While the profit margin of USD 0.0005 may seem to be very small, if the deal was for, say, USD 10 million, the profit will be USD 5,000- *on a completely risk-free basis.*

Let us take an example of an arbitrage opportunity between different forex markets.

Suppose, in New York, the following exchange rates are being quoted as:

1 GBP = 1.3518 USD, and

1 EUR = 1.1792 USD.

And suppose, at the same time, the EUR to GBP rate in London is 0.8721, can you do an arbitrage operation? Yes, you can.

Given the GBP to USD and EUR to USD rates given in New York, we can derive the prevailing EUR to GBP rate in New York, as 1.1792 ÷ 1.3518, ie., 0.8723.

Now, this EUR to GBP rate is slightly different from 0.8721 prevailing in London at the same time. Thus, in London, 1 EUR buys 0.8721 GBP, which is lesser that 0.8723 GBP that 1 EUR can buy in New York.

Hence, the EUR is weaker in London than in New York, which may be due to some intrinsic distorting local factor in Europe, say, like poor GDP growth figures released by one of the major EU countries, like Germany.

At this point of time, therefore, there is an anomaly through which it is possible to make arbitrage profit.

So, if I have 1 GBP in New York, I can sell it to buy 1.3518 USD.

I can use this 1.3518 USD to buy (1.1793 ÷ 1.3518), ie., 0.8724 EUR

And, in the London market, I can sell the 0.8724 EUR to buy (0.8724 ÷ 0.8721), ie., 1.0034 GBP.

Consequently, having started with 1 GBP, I have ended with GBP 1.0034, and thereby, made a small profit of GBP 0.0034.

These transactions are depicted in the following figure.

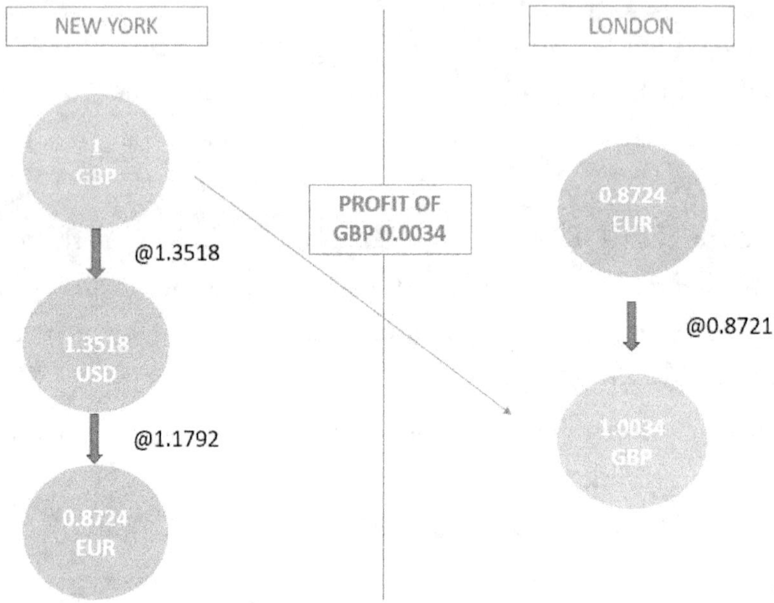

Figure 4.4 Arbitrage Operations

Accordingly, seeing the arbitrage opportunity, if I had sold GBP 1 million in New York, I would have ended up with a profit of (1,000,000 x 0.0034), ie., **GBP 3,400 profit.**

This arbitrage opportunity, however, will not last for long. Seeing the opportunity, the demand for EUR in London will go up, which will strengthen the EUR and the rate of EUR to GBP will increase from 0.8721 to 0.8724 – which is the level in London, and an equation where there is zero profit.

Further strengthening of EUR in London will cease, since once it strengthens beyond 0.8724 (say, 0.8725), the arbitrage trade will start leading into loss.

EXERCISE 4

1. What is the total daily turnover in the global forex market?

   a. USD 6.6 Tn

   b. USD 7.5 Tn

   c. USD 9.6 Tn

2. What percentage of forex transactions involves the US Dollar?

   a. 56%

   b. 88%

   c. 94%

3. Which of the following centres accounts for maximum number of forex trades?

   a. London

   b. New York

   c. Tokyo

4. Which of the following is the first major forex market to open?

   a. Auckland

   b. Sydney

   c. Tokyo

5. Which of the following centres is the last major forex market to open?

   a. London

   b. New York

   c. San Francisco

6. If the Non-Farm Payroll data announced in USA turns out to be weaker than expected, what would be the likely effect on the US Dollar?

   a. USD will weaken

   b. USD will strengthen

   c. There will be no effect on USD

7. Which of the following is the most active player in the forex market?

   a. Governments

   b. Central banks

   c. Commercial banks

8. Mr Mehta, who is an NRI, has placed INR 10 lakhs in NRE deposit for a period of 1 year, with Commercial Bank, Mumbai branch. In order to reduce his risk to foreign exchange fluctuations, he books a forward contract for 1 year.

   In which of the following categories can Mr Mehta be classified?

a. Speculator

b. Arbitrageur

c. Hedger

9. The following exchange rates are prevailing in New York, Frankfurt and London:

   GBP 1 = USD 1.4110 (in New York)

   EUR 1 = USD 1.1850 (in Frankfurt)

   EUR 1 = GBP 0.9000 (in London)

   Given the above rates, is there any arbitrage opportunity?

   a. Yes

   b. No

10. The following exchange rates are prevailing in Tokyo, Hongkong and Singapore:

    USD 1 = JPY 144.22 (in Tokyo)

    USD 1 = HKD 7.8200 (in Hongkong)

    JPY 1 = HKD 0.0600 (in Singapore)

    Given the above rates, is there any arbitrage opportunity?

    a. Yes

    b. No

Chapter 5

Commodity Nature of Foreign Currencies

5.1 BUYERS AND SELLERS OF FOREIGN CURRENCY

Foreign exchange, as you have studied, is primarily required to facilitate international trade, as well as facilitate international money transfers. Exporters and importers require foreign exchange. So would an Indian tourist who is travelling to a foreign country on a holiday or a foreign tourist who is visiting India on a holiday.

Which types of persons would buy foreign currency? An importer would be in this category since the importer would require foreign currency to pay for his / her imports. So, also an individual wanting to, say, remit college fees for his child's education in a foreign university.

Such customers would require to buy foreign currency. In India, foreign currency can be bought and sold to customers only by commercial banks, and in some types of transactions, by money changers. Hence, such customers would require to BUY their foreign currency from a commercial bank and a commercial bank would SELL the foreign currency to such a customer.

Which types of persons would sell foreign currency? An exporter would be in this category since the exporter would require to sell the foreign currency that he / she receives as payment for the exports. So also, an individual who has received a foreign currency remittance from his / her relatives or a person who had earlier bought foreign currency for travelling abroad but could not spend it completely and now needs to surrender the unspent portion.

Hence, such customers would require to SELL their foreign currency to a commercial bank and the commercial bank would, in turn, BUY the foreign currency from such customers.

To sum up, therefore,

- Customers who need to buy foreign exchange from a commercial bank are importers, senders of outward remittances and Indian tourists intending to travel abroad and, therefore, need foreign currency notes and / or travel cards, and
- Customers who need to sell foreign exchange to a commercial bank are exporters, receivers of inward remittances, foreign tourists visiting India and Indian tourists who have returned from abroad with unspent foreign exchange.

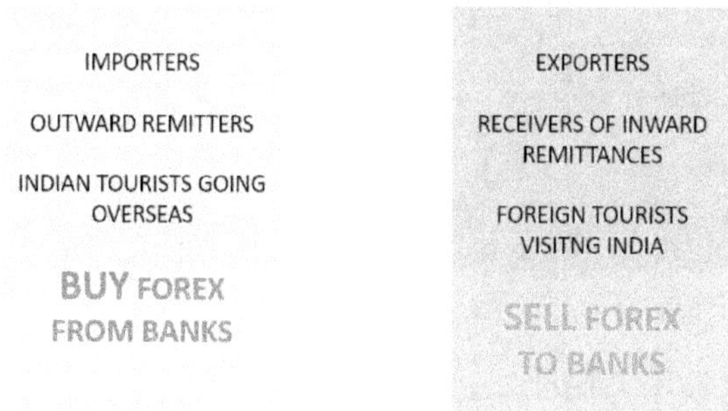

Figure 5.1 Customers as Buyers and Sellers of Forex

Check Your Understanding

5.1 Which of the following entities would be buyers of foreign currency?

a. Importers

b. Exporters

c. A foreign student in India, receiving maintenance expenses from his parents in Germany

d. Titus Ltd, which has decided to put an advertisement, in a magazine published from Singapore

e. Mr Chavan, who is remitting fees of AUD 10,000- to a University in Australia for education of his daughter

f. An American tourist encashing USD 500 in a hotel in Varanasi

g. A housewife in Kochi receiving a draft for INR 10,000- from her husband who is employed in Dubai

Answer: a, d, e.

Check Your Understanding

5.2 Which of the following entities would be sellers of foreign currency?

a. Importers

b. Exporters

c. A foreign student in India, receiving maintenance expenses from his parents in Germany

d. Titus Ltd, which has decided to put an advertisement, in a magazine published from Singapore

e. Mr Chavan, who is remitting fees of AUD 10,000- to a University in Australia for education of his daughter

f. An American tourist encashing USD 500 in a hotel in Varanasi

g. A housewife in Kochi receiving a draft for INR 10,000- from her husband who is employed in Dubai

Answer: b, c, f, g.

5.2 REVERSAL OF ROLE FOR BANKS

From the perspective of the Bank, the roles are reversed and can be represented as in the figure below.

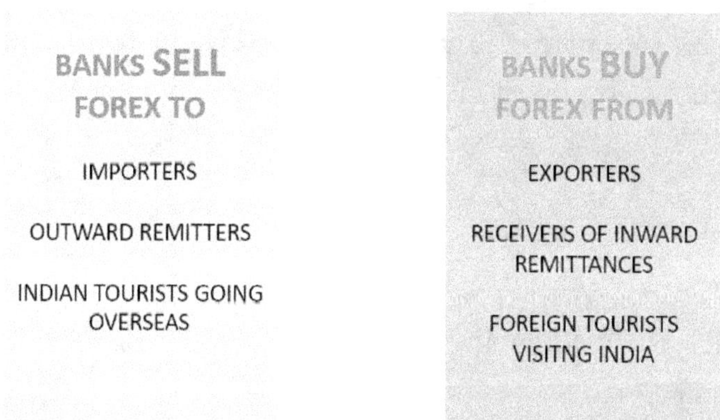

Figure 5.2 Banks as Sellers and Buyers of Forex

Check Your Understanding

5.3 Which of the following cases would a bank be a buyer of foreign currency?

a. Handling an import transaction

b. Handling an export transaction

c. Crediting proceeds of an inward remittance for a foreign student in India, who has received maintenance expenses from his parents in Germany

d. Making a remittance on account of its customer, Titus Ltd, which has decided to put an advertisement, in a magazine published from Singapore

e. Making a transfer of AUD 10,000- to a University in Australia for its customer, Mr Chavan, who is remitting fees for education of his daughter

f. Encashing USD 500 currency notes from an American tourist in Varanasi

g. Crediting proceeds of a draft of INR 10,000- to the account of a housewife in Kochi who has received it from her husband who is employed in Dubai.

Answer: b, c, f, g.

Check Your Understanding

5.4 Which of the following cases would a bank be a seller of foreign currency?

a. Handling an import transaction

b. Handling an export transaction

c. Crediting proceeds of an inward remittance for a foreign student in India, who has received maintenance expenses from his parents in Germany

d. Making a remittance on account of its customer, Titus Ltd, which has decided to put an advertisement, in a magazine published from Singapore

e. Making a transfer of AUD 10,000- to a University in Australia for its customer, Mr Chavan, who is remitting fees for education of his daughter

f. Encashing USD 500 currency notes from an American tourist in Varanasi

g. Crediting proceeds of a draft of INR 10,000- to the account of a housewife in Kochi who has received it from her husband who is employed in Dubai

Answer: a, d, e.

EXERCISE 5

1. Mr Anand is expecting to receive a gift of Canadian Dollars (CAD) 100- from his uncle in Toronto.

   Which of the following is appropriate with respect to him being a buyer or seller of foreign exchange?

   a. Buyer

   b. Seller

2. Bank of Kottayam has received a request from Sailesh Exports to refund USD 10,000- which has been claimed by the foreign buyer.

   Which of the following is appropriate with respect to the Bank being a buyer or seller of foreign exchange?

   a. Buyer

   b. Seller

3. Commercial Bank has received a request from its customer to issue a pre-paid forex card with a limit of USD 5,000-.

   Which of the following is appropriate with respect to the customer being a buyer or seller of foreign exchange?

   a. Buyer

   b. Seller

4. The captain of the Indian cricket team has received an award amounting to GBP 50,000- from International Cricket Council for his performance in the recent Test series. -.

   Which of the following is appropriate with respect to the player being a buyer or seller of foreign exchange?

   a. Buyer

   b. Seller

5. Mr Khanna has bought a pre-paid forex card for USD 5,000- which he used in Europe when he was there on vacation. After his return to India, he found that the card still had a balance of USD 125- in the card, and he visited his bank requesting for crediting the amount to his account.

   Which of the following is appropriate with respect to the Bank being a buyer or seller of foreign exchange?

   a. Buyer

   b. Seller

6. Mr Rohit had purchased a demand draft for Australian Dollars (AUD) 2,000- for meeting the college fees of his son, who was pursuing an academic course in Melbourne. However, he has now found out that the DD is no longer required by the College and he has approached his banker to cancel the draft.

   Which of the following is appropriate with respect to Mr Rohit being a buyer or seller of foreign exchange?

   a. Buyer

   b. Seller

7. Alpha Imports had made an advance payment amounting to EUR 32,000- to its suppliers in France for import of a machinery item. However, owing to strike in France, the supplier could not fulfil the order and has returned the advance payment, along with interest at 2% pa.

   Which of the following is appropriate with respect to Alpha Imports being a buyer or seller of foreign exchange?

   a. Buyer

   b. Seller

8. Alpha Imports has requested its bankers to remit an amount of Singapore Dollars (SGD) 25,000- being cost of electronic components purchased by it from Liu Digitals, Singapore.

   Which of the following is appropriate with respect to the Bank being a buyer or seller of foreign exchange?

   a. Buyer

   b. Seller

Chapter 6

Types of Foreign Exchange Quotations

6.1 DIRECT AND INDIRECT QUOTES

Exchange rates can be quoted in two different manners – Direct and Indirect.

What is today's INR USD rate? 90.10? WRONG……

What is today's USD INR rate? 90.10? RIGHT!! (and the correct INR USD rate is 0.0110 !!)

So, what is the difference between USD INR and INR USD conventions? There is a lot of difference.

USD INR is a Direct Quotation of the exchange rate, whereas INR USD is an Indirect Quotation of the exchange rate.

In direct quotation, the price of one unit the foreign currency is quoted in terms of the number of units of the domestic currency.

Say, 1 USD = INR 90.10.

It is observed that in direct quotation, the number of units of foreign currency (USD) is fixed (1 unit), whereas the number of units of domestic currency (INR) is variable (INR 90 or INR 90.10, etc.).

This is quite similar to saying 1 apple = INR 25.

On the contrary, in an indirect quotation, it is the reverse. Here, the number of units of domestic currency is fixed, say 1 Rupee and the number of units of foreign currency is variable.

For example, 100 INR = USD 1.1100

[For calculating the indirect rate for INR, the market convention is to use 100 INR as the unit and not 1 INR, because the INR is a small currency, value-wise. So is the case of the Japanese Yen.]

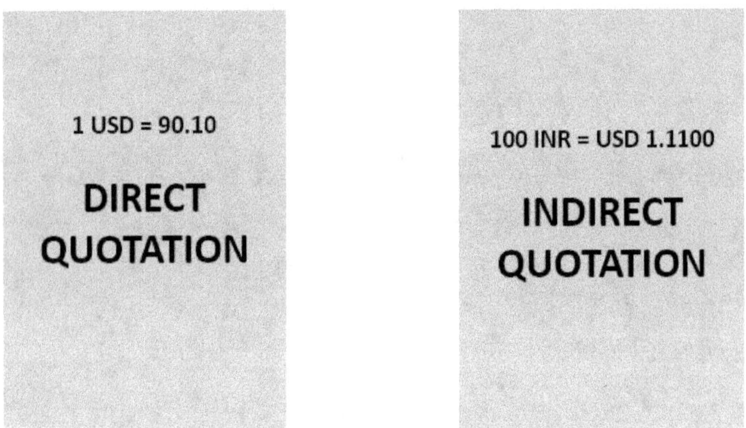

Figure 6.1 Direct and Indirect Quotes

Looking at a similar example from our now popular fruit market,

INR 100 = 4 apples

It can also be seen that the indirect rate is a reciprocal of the direct rate, that is when USD INR rate is 90.20, the indirect rate, INR USD = (1 ÷ 90.20) = 1.1086 (for 100 Rupees).

The currency on the left-hand side is called the BASE CURRENCY whereas the currency on the right-hand side is called the QUOTED CURRENCY.

Hence, 1 USD = INR 90.10
(BASE) (QUOTED)

To sum up, therefore:

DIRECT QUOTE		***INDIRECT QUOTE***
Foreign currency is quoted in terms of domestic currency units.		Domestic currency is quoted in terms of foreign currency units.
IN INDIA		IN INDIA
1 USD = INR 90.10	AND	100 INR = USD 1.1100
IN JAPAN		IN LONDON
1 USD = JPY 145		1 GBP = USD 1.35
IN BAZAR		IN BAZAR
I APPLE = INR 25		100 INR = 4 APPLES

The currency on the left is called the Base Currency whereas the currency on the right is called the Quoted Currency.

Check Your Understanding

6.1 In India, JPY INR is quoted at 56.62. This is an example of a / an:

a. Direct quote

b. Indirect quote

Answer: a

Check Your Understanding

6.2 In London, GBP USD is quoted at 1.1110. This is an example of a / an:

a. Direct quote

b. Indirect quote

Answer: b

Check Your Understanding

6.3 If USD INR is quoted as 89.90, what will its indirect quote (in terms of INR 100)?

a. 90.10

b. 1.1099

c. 1.1123

d. There cannot be an indirect rate

Answer: c

Check Your Understanding

6.4 In the fruit market, oranges are selling at Rs 200 per dozen. This is an example of a / an:

a. Direct rate

b. Indirect rate

Answer: b

Check Your Understanding

6.5 In the New York market, Canadian Dollar is quoted as USD CAD = 1.3624. This is an example of a / an:

a. Direct rate

b. Indirect rate

Answer: b

6.2 TWO WAY QUOTES – MARKET MAKER AND MARKET TAKER

Let us understand the role of a commercial bank in India, in the context of foreign exchange transactions. It is the customers of the Bank who need to buy and sell foreign currencies. For example, exporters, importers, senders and receivers of remittances, depositors, etc. However, such customers cannot buy and sell foreign exchange without the intermediation of a commercial bank (or, in some types of cases, a money changer.)

If an importer wants to buy USD, it must do so through its banker. The bank will buy USD from the forex market using the INR made available by importer, and then provide the USD (sell it) to the importer.

Similarly, if an exporter wants to sell USD and get INR, it must do so through its banker. The bank will buy USD from the exporter and then sell the USD in the foreign exchange market and then pass on the INR that the bank receives from the market, to the exporter.

The bank, technically, starts with a zero-forex position in the morning. It buys and sells foreign currencies throughout the day for its customers and would like to end the day with a zero position. The bank would not like to close the day with a "over-bought" position or with a "over-sold" position, as that would attract risk of loss due to fluctuations in the forex rates during the time the bank is closed for the night.

[Note: Over-bought position means that the bank has bought more of the foreign currency than it has sold. Over-sold position means that the bank has sold more of the foreign currency than it has bought.]

As seen above, it is the commercial bank which buys and sells foreign exchange from the forex market for its customers. But, from whom in the forex market? From the Government or the RBI? No. It buys and sells foreign currency in the forex markets from / to other commercial banks. Hence, banks buy / sell from / to its customers and also sells / buys to / from other banks in the forex market.

This brings us to the concept of Market Maker and Market Taker, which is explained by using the following two examples.

Example - 1

ABC Imports requires USD 100,000 for making a payment for goods imported by it. It requires USD and, therefore, approaches its bank, say, Commercial Bank. It has adequate INR in its current account for buying USD 100,000. Now, Commercial Bank does not have any USD as it has closed yesterday's position at zero. So, it enters the forex market (using its computerised Reuter terminal) and seeks a quote from other banks in the market for USD.

Now, the other bank which is in the forex market, say, International Bank, does not know whether Commercial Bank already has USD and wants to sell it or whether it requires USD and wants to buy USD.

Hence, International Bank gives a TWO-WAY Quote for the USD, say, USD INR = 90.00 / 90.10.

The above quote means that International Bank is willing to BUY USD from Commercial Bank (or any other bank, at that time) at a rate of 90.00 and it is willing to SELL USD to Commercial Bank (or any other bank, at that time) at 90.10. A Bank like International Bank, giving a two-way quote is called a **Market Maker**, and the transaction is called an **Inter-Bank transaction** since both the parties in the forex market transaction are banks.

Why is the buying rate and selling rate quoted by International Bank different (90.00 and 90.10)? This is so that International Bank can buy USD at 90.00 and sell USD at 90.10, and make a profit of INR 0.10 for every USD.

Now, Commercial Bank needs to buy USD 100,000 for its customer ABC Imports. Hence, it buys USD 100,000 from International Bank.

At what rate?

It can buy USD 100,000 from International Bank at International Bank's selling rate, that is 90.10. Therefore, Commercial Bank buys USD 100,000 from International Bank @ 90.10 and pays it INR 90,10,000-.

From where does it get INR to pay International Bank? From the current account of ABC Imports who required the USD 100,000- to meet its import payment.

You will observe that while International Bank quoted two rates (90.00 and 90.10) to Commercial Bank, Commercial Bank will quote only one rate, viz., 90.10 to its customer ABC Imports.

Commercial Bank, in this example, is called the **Market Taker** and the transaction is called a **Merchant transaction** as it is between a bank and its customer (Merchant).

[Of course, in the above merchant transaction, if Commercial Bank sells the USD 100,000 to ABC Imports @ 90.10, it will make no profit. It will, therefore, **add** a profit margin of, say INR 0.20 to the inter-bank rate and effectively sell it at 90.30 (90.10 + 0.20 = 90.30) to ABC Imports. 90.10, in this example is called the Inter-Bank rate and 90.30 is called the Merchant rate.]

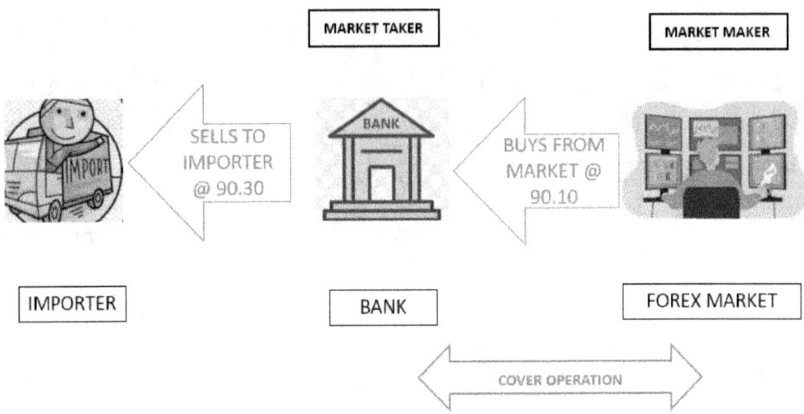

Figure 6.2 Meeting requirement of the importer

Example - 2

XYZ Exports has received USD 500,000 as proceeds of an export made by it a few months ago. It requires INR and, therefore, approaches its bank, say, Commercial Bank. In order that Commercial Bank can provide INR to XYZ Exports, it must sell the USD 500,000 in the inter-bank market. So, it enters the forex market (using its computerised Reuter terminal) and seeks a quote from other banks in the forex market for USD.

As in the earlier example, the other bank, say, International Bank, does not know whether Commercial Bank already has USD and wants to sell it or whether it requires USD and wants to buy it. Hence, International Bank gives a TWO-WAY Quote for the USD, say, USD INR = 90.00 / 90.10.

Commercial Bank needs to sell USD 500,000 on behalf of its customer XYZ Exports. Hence, it sells USD 500,000 to International Bank in the inter-bank market.

At what rate?

Commercial Bank can sell USD 500,000 to International Bank at International Bank's buying rate, that is 90.00. So, Commercial Bank sells USD 500,000 to International Bank @ 90.00 and receives INR 4,50,00,000- from it and credits the INR amount to the current account of XYZ Exports.

In this example, too, Commercial Bank is the Market Taker, and International Bank is the Market Maker.

[Of course, in the above merchant transaction, if Commercial Bank buys the USD 500,000 from XYZ Exports @ 90.00, it will make no profit. It will, therefore, **deduct** a profit margin of, say INR 0.20 from the inter-bank rate and effectively buy it at 89.80 (90.00 - 0.20 – 89.80) to XYZ Exports. 90.00, in this example is the Inter-Bank rate and 89.80 is the Merchant rate.]

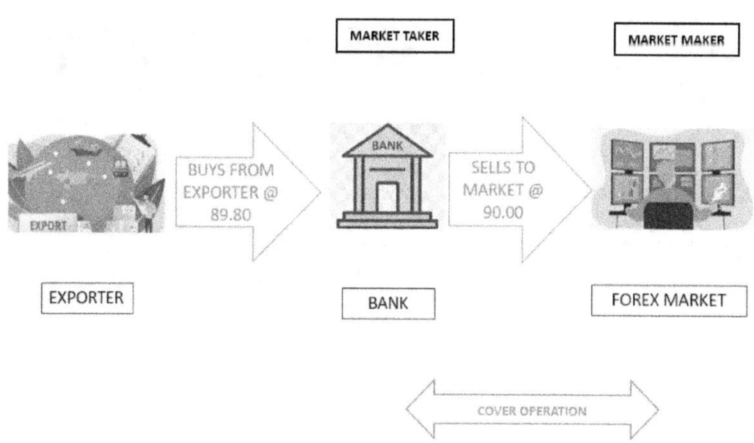

Figure 6.3 Meeting requirement of the exporter

Fron the above examples, it is observed that in all interbank transactions, the quote is two-way.

For example:

USD INR = 90.00 / 90.10

Some terminologies:

In the above quote, 90.00 is the buying rate or **BID rate** and 90.10 is the selling rate or the **ASK rate**, also known as **OFFER rate.**

The difference of INR 0.10 between the buying and selling rates, is called the **SPREAD** and it constitutes the profit margin for the Market Making bank.

When a bank (in these examples, Commercial Bank) enters the interbank market to BUY or SELL foreign currencies because of an underlying request of its customer (merchant), that operation of undertaking an inter-bank transaction is known as a **COVER OPERATION**.

Check Your Understanding

6.6 An importer has to make payment of USD 50,000 to its German supplier. The interbank rate prevailing for USD INR is 89.75 / 89.85. Which of the foregoing rates will be applicable to this transaction?

a. 89.75

b. 89.85

Answer: b

Check Your Understanding

6.7 Mr Joseph has received a wire transfer of USD 1,500 from his brother in New Zealand. The interbank rate prevailing for USD INR is 90.75 / 90.85. Which of the foregoing rates will be applicable to this transaction?

a. 90.75

b. 90.85

Answer: a

Check Your Understanding

6.8 Phoenix Shipping Co. is required to remit USD 150,000- as insurance premium to Lloyds International, London. The interbank rate prevailing for USD INR is 89.75 / 89.85. Which of the foregoing rates will be applicable to this transaction?

a. 89.75

b. 89.85

Answer: b

Check Your Understanding

6.9 Mr Ganesh wants to visit Iceland to see the Northern Lights in winter. For his tour to Iceland, he has to pay USD 15,000- to Deluxe Travels and Tours, Paris.

The interbank rate prevailing for USD INR is 90.75 / 90.85. Which of the foregoing rates will be applicable to this transaction?

a. 90.75

b. 90.85

Answer: b

6.3 WHAT DETERMINES THE SPREAD?

In the example given in this chapter, the spread was assumed to be INR 0.10, ie., 10 paise. The spread may be, either expressed in paise, or it may be expressed as a percentage, like 0.25%, etc.

How small or large a spread is, will be depend upon a number of factors.

Basically, if the currency pair is a well traded one, with the currencies being fully convertible and the market for the pair is deep, the spread will be small.

However, if the market receives a sudden jolt, due to some geo-political crisis or some bad news, the spread can immediately increase as the risk in the market will have increased.

Hence, in such a condition, the USD INR quote of 90.00 / 90.10 can immediately change to, say, 90.00 / 90.20 (spread of 20 paise) or 90.00 / 90.35 (spread of 35 paise).

Small spread is also known as 'fine' spread, whereas large spread is also known as 'wide' spread.

Figure 6.4 Spreads – small (fine) and large (wide)

6.4 WHY DOES THE SPREAD INCREASE OR DECREASE?

What, after all, is spread? As you have already learnt, spread constitutes the bank's profit margin. Whenever a condition arises that increases the riskiness of the forex market, banks would try to play safe and increase their profit margins so that they can counter the heightened risks. Therefore, the spread will increase (or widen).

On the contrary, when the market is calm, the level of risk is subdued. In such situations, banks do not need to keep large profit margins and can, instead, carry on their operations with lesser profit margins. Therefore, the spread decreases (or narrows)

Check Your Understanding

6.10 USD INR is being quoted in the interbank market at 89.65 / 89.75. Calculate the spread in the quote.

a. INR 0.65

b. INR 0.75

c. INR 0.10

Answer: c

Check Your Understanding

6.11 USD INR is being quoted in the interbank market at 90.00 / 90.10. Calculate the spread in the quote.

a. INR 0.10

b. INR 0.20

c. No spread

Answer: a

Check Your Understanding

6.12 In a sudden attack on Israeli settlements, radical forces unleash a barrage of rockets and shells. The interbank USD INR is quoting at 83.20 / 83.25.

Is the spread expected to increase, decrease or remain the same?

a. Increase

b. Decrease

c. Remain the same

Answer: a

6.5 FOREX BUYING AND SELLING MAXIMS

You have learnt that banks provide two-way quotes, which consist of two rates – one at which the bank will buy foreign currency and the other at which it will sell the foreign currency.

At which of the two rates a bank will buy or sell, depends upon whether the quote is a direct quote, or it is an indirect quote.

Let us presume that the quote for USD Dollar, against INR is as follows:

Direct Quote – USD = 90.00 / 90.20 INR

Indirect quote – USD = 1.1111 / 1.1086 for INR 100

When the quote is direct, the Maxim is **"BUY LOW, SELL HIGH"** and when the quote is indirect, the Maxim is **"BUY HIGH, SELL LOW"**.

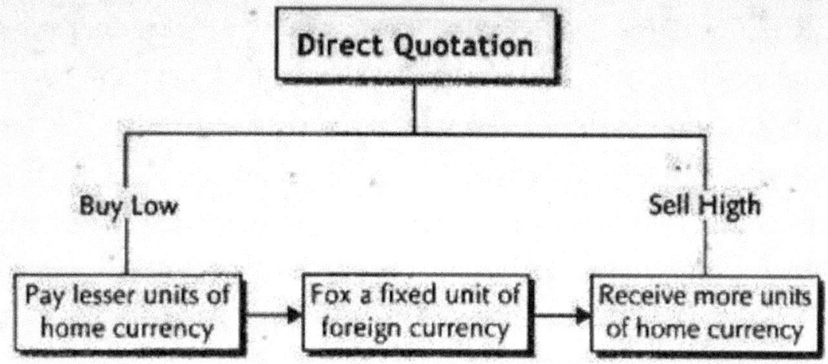

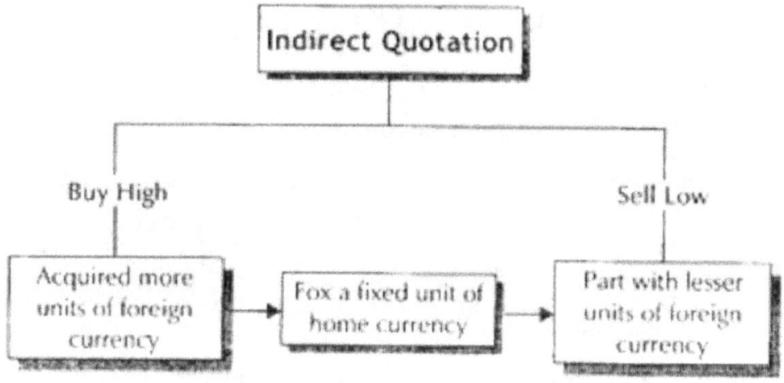

Figure 6.5 Buying and Selling Maxims

Hence, in the case of direct quote, the bank will BUY USD at 90.00 and will SELL USD at 90.20, whereas in the case of indirect quote, the bank will BUY USD 1.1111 for every INR 100, and will SELL USD 1.1086 for every INR 100.

To understand the above maxim properly, let us equate it to buying apples, where the quotes are:

Direct Quote – Apples = 20.00 / 25.00 INR

Indirect Quote – Apples = 5 / 4 for INR 100

In the first quote, you will buy apples at Rs 20 and sell apples at Rs 25, whereas in the second quote, you will BUY at a price of 5 apples for every Rs 100, and SELL at a price of 4 apples for every Rs 100.

In India, prior to August 1993, the convention in the forex market was to have Indirect Quotes. This was changed to Direct Quotes from August, 1993.

Check Your Understanding

6.13 In the Indian market, USD INR is quoted at 89.95 / 90.05. As what rate can USD be sold against INR?

a. 90.05

b. 89.95

Answer: b

Check Your Understanding

6.14 In the Indian market, USD INR is quoted at 89.75 / 89.80. As what rate can INR be sold against USD?

a. 89.75

b. 89.80

Answer: b

[Note: In a USD INR quote, selling INR against USD is the same as buying USD against INR]

Check Your Understanding

6.15 In the London market, EUR USD is quoted at 1.1200 / 1.1225. As what rate can USD be sold against EUR?

a. 1.1200

b. 1.1225

Answer: b

Check Your Understanding

6.16 In the Frankfurt market, EUR USD is quoted at 1.1850 / 1.1875. At what rate can USD be bought against EUR?

a. 1.1850

b. 1.1875 *

Answer: b

6.6 BASE CURRENCIES AND QUOTED CURRENCIES – MAJOR CURRENCIES

You have already learnt about the terminology of Base currency and Quoted currency. The currency, whose symbol appears on the left is the Base currency, whereas the currency whose symbol appears on the right is the Quoted currency.

For example, in the following currency pairs,

EUR USD (EUR Base – USD Quoted)

USD JPY (USD Base – JPY Quoted)

The question that arises, therefore, is that in any currency pair which currency should be the Base currency and which currency should be the Quoted currency.

For example, whereas in USD INR quotes, USD is the Base currency, in GBP USD quotes, USD becomes the Quoted currency.

USD INR (**USD Base** – INR Quoted)

GBP USD (GBP Base – **USD Quoted**)

To resolve this situation, there is an international convention which recognises the following eight currencies as major currencies, in the following order:

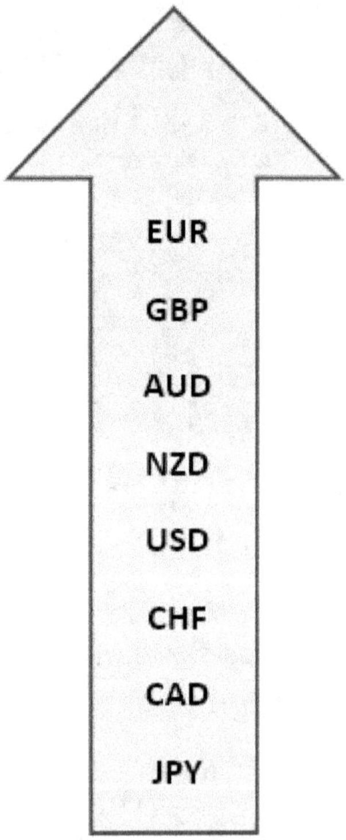

Figure 6.6 Order of Major Currencies

The highest major currency in the aforesaid group is EUR and the lowest major currency in the group is JPY. The market convention is that –

When any pair of currencies is quoted, the major currency is always the Base currency. For example, USD INR, EUR INR, CHF INR, etc. (As can be seen, USD, EUR and CHF are major currencies, whereas INR is not a major currency).

Then what will happen if both the currencies in the pair are major currencies, for example, US Dollars and Euros?

When both the currencies in the quoted pair are major currencies, the currency which is higher up on the arrow will become the Base currency, and the currency which is lower on the arrow will become the Quoted currency.

For example, EUR-GBP, GBP-AUD, GBP-USD, USD-CHF, CHF-CAD, etc.

Check Your Understanding

6.17 Which of the following is the correct manner for quotes of USD against CAD?

a. USD CAD

b. CAD USD

Answer: a

Check Your Understanding

6.18 Which of the following is the correct manner for quotes of AUD against NZD?

a. NZD AUD

b. AUD NZD

Answer: b

Check Your Understanding

6.19 Which of the following is the correct manner for quotes of EUR against GBP?

a. GBP EUR

b. EUR GBP

Answer: b

Check Your Understanding

6.20 Which of the following is the correct manner for quotes of HKD against CHF?

a. HKD CHF

b. CHF HKD

Answer: b

Check Your Understanding

6.21 Which of the following is the correct manner for quotes of SGD against AUD?

a. AUD SGD

b. SGD AUD

Answer: a

EXERCISE 6

1. Quoting an exchange rate like INR USD = 1.1111, in Mumbai, is an example of which type of quote?

   a. Direct

   b. Indirect

2. In Paris, the quote USD EUR = 0.8546 is an example of which type of quote?

   a. Direct

   b. Indirect

3. A price in the fruit market of Rs 200 per a dozen of apples is an example of which type of quote?

   a. Direct

   b. Indirect

4. In foreign exchange, direct quotes are a reciprocal of the indirect quotes. Is this statement true or false?

   a. True

   b. False

5. Mr Roy has requested his bank to remit USD 15,000- to an American University towards tuition fees for his son. The ruling USD INR interbank rate is 90.6650 / 90.6675.

   Which of the two interbank rates will be reckoned for the bankers of Mr Roy to calculate the merchant rate for the said transaction?

   a. 90.6650

   b. 90.6675

6. In the Tokyo market, the US Dollar is quoting at 144.50 / 145.50. which out of the two rates is the bid rate?

   a. 144.50

   b. 145.50

7. In London market, EUR USD is quoting at 1.1922 / 1.1940. which of the two rates in the ask rate?

   a. 1.1922

   b. 1.1940

8. In the Singapore market, USD SGD = 1.2880 / 1.2905. There is a news announcement that a huge volcano has erupted in the South Pacific. What effect is this event expected to have on the spread?

   a. Spread will increase

   b. Spread will decrease

   c. There will be no impact on the spread

9. During the recent Iran Israeli war, it has been announced that United Nations will form a committee to take charge of the situation in order to curtail the oil prices. What will be impact of this announcement on the spread in GBP USD spread?

   a. Spread will increase

   b. Spread will decrease

   c. There will be no impact on the spread

10. In the London market, EUR USD is quoting at 1.2020 / 1.2025.

    What will be the maxim for a bank which wants to buy USD against EUR?

    a, Buy high

    b. Buy low

    c. Neither of the above

11. In the London market, EUR USD is quoting at 1.2020 / 1.2025.

    What will be the maxim for a bank which wants to buy EUR against USD?

    a. Buy high

    b. Buy low

    c. Neither of the above

Chapter 7

Calculation of Merchant Rates

7.1 WHAT IS A MERCHANT RATE

When a bank's customer makes a request to buy foreign currency (for example, an importer) or to sell foreign currency (for example, an exporter), the bank must quote it the appropriate exchange rate.

Let us consider that the foreign currency for which exchange rate has to be quoted to the customer (merchant rate) is USD. How does the bank arrive at the correct rate?

Here, you have to remember, that the bank does not, normally, keep any balance of foreign currency and, hence, if the customer wants to buy USD, the bank must buy USD from the market at the prevailing interbank SELLING rate and give it to the customer.

Similarly, if the customer wants to sell USD, the bank must, further, sell the USD in the market at the interbank BUYING rate.

Accordingly, the bank must know what the interbank buying and selling rates are, in order that it can work out a suitable rate for its customer.

The interbank rate is, thus, the primary rate based on which the merchant rate is calculated. It is like the wholesale rate. To this rate, an amount of margin of profit is also loaded.

In convention, the terminology of using terms "BUY" and "SELL" is with relation to the bank and not the merchant. Hence, if an exporter wants to sell USD, the bank will buy it and hence the bank will quote its Merchant BUYING rate. On the other hand, if an importer wants to buy USD, the bank will have to sell the USD to the importer and will, therefore, quote its Merchant SELLING rate.

7.2 CALCULATION OF MERCHANT BUYING RATE

Let us use an example to understand how to calculate the Merchant Buying Rate.

Example: Cosmic Exports has received USD 250,000- on export of rice to USA. It requires INR equivalent of the USD 250,000- and approaches its bank, say, Commercial Bank for USD INR rate.

The interbank USD INR rate, ruling at that time, quoted by International Bank is 90.2525 / 3075 (Means 90.2525 / 90.3075).

As you have already learnt, 90.2525 is the interbank buying rate (the rate at which International Bank is agreeable to buy USD against INR) and 90.3075 is the interbank selling rate (the rate at which International Bank is agreeable to sell USD against INR).

Commercial Bank is going to buy USD 250,000- from Cosmic Exports and pay it INR. Hence, Commercial Bank will have to sell the USD 250,000- in the interbank market to International Bank, and International Bank will BUY USD 250,000- from Commercial Bank at its BUYING rate, ie., 90.2525.

Let us presume that Commercial Bank has a policy to keep a profit margin of 0.45%.

The Merchant Buying rate is calculated as follows:

Interbank buying rate	90.2525
LESS profit margin (0.45% on 90.2525)	0.4061
	89.8464
∴ Merchant Buying Rate	89.84

The merchant buying rate that will be quoted by Commercial Bank to Cosmic Exports is 89.84.

In order to understand the above calculation, the following aspects should be noted:

a. *Why is profit margin loaded?*

   It is loaded because the bank would aspire to book profit on every forex transaction that it undertakes with the merchant.

b. *Why is profit margins deducted, instead of being added to the interbank rate?*

   That is because, when Commercial Bank is quoting its Merchant Buying rate, it is based on the presumption that it will sell the USD in the interbank market buying rate.

   If the margin was to be added, the bank would quote a higher buying rate to the exporter, thereby paying more INR to the exporter than it would receive from the interbank sale and incurring a loss in the transaction.

   The rule is, therefore, that when a bank like Commercial bank quotes merchant buying rate, it must deduct the profit margin.

   (The opposite would be case when the bank quotes its merchant selling rate, as you will see in the following example).

c. *Why is the merchant rate (arrived at 89.8464) reduced to 89.84 and not rounded off to 89.85?*

That is because, in order to protect its profit, the bank would like to give as few INR to the exporter, as possible. Consider the situation where the merchant rate is 89.85 versus 89.84.

89.85 – Commercial Bank will pay INR 2,24,62,500– to the exporter

89.84 - Commercial Bank will pay INR 2,24,60,000– to the exporter

Obviously, Commercial Bank would like to pay INR 2,24,60,000 to the exporter rather than INR ,24,62,500 and, hence, would quote the lower rate of 89.84.

d. *Why is the merchant rate quoted in 2 decimal places, whereas the interbank rate is quoted in 4 decimal places?*

Because, that is the convention in India.

e. The abovementioned flow for calculation of merchant buying rate is depicted in the following figure:

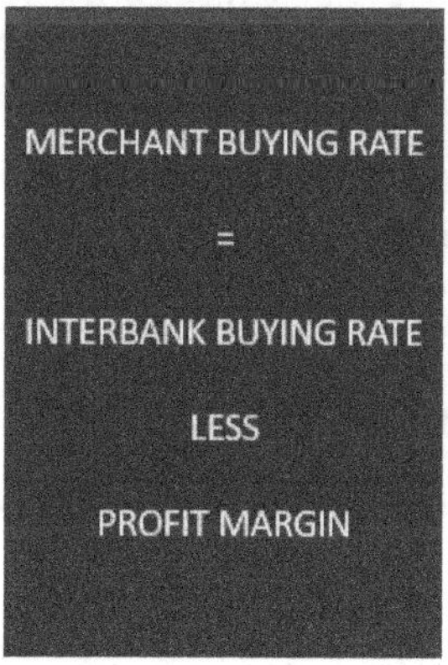

Figure 7.1 Calculation of merchant buying rate

7.3 CALCULATION OF MERCHANT SELLING RATE

Let us use the following example to understand how to calculate the Merchant Selling Rate.

Example: Prism Imports has to make payment of USD 300,000- for import of a machinery that it has purchased from Singapore. It has INR in its current account for the USD 300,000- it wants to buy, and approaches its bank, Commercial Bank for USD INR rate.

The interbank USD INR rate, ruling at that time, quoted by International Bank is 90.2525 / 3075.

As you have already learnt, 90.2525 is the interbank buying rate (the rate at which International Bank is agreeable to buy USD against INR) and 90.3075 is the interbank selling rate (the rate at which International Bank is agreeable to sell USD against INR).

Commercial Bank is going to buy USD 300,000- for Prism Imports and recover the INR amount from the current account of the importer. Commercial Bank will, therefore, have to BUY the USD 300,000- from International Bank in the interbank market, and International Bank will SELL USD 300,000- to Commercial Bank at its SELLING rate, 90.3075.

Let us presume that Commercial Bank has a policy to keep a profit margin of 0.50%.

The Merchant Selling rate is calculated as follows:

Interbank selling rate	90.3075
ADD profit margin (0.50% on 90.3075)	0.4515
	90.7590

∴ Merchant Selling Rate	90.76

The merchant selling rate that Commercial Bank will quote to Prism Imports is 90.76.

In order to understand the above calculation, the following aspects should be noted, in addition to points elaborated in the last section:

a. *Why is profit margins being added to the interbank rate, instead of being deducted?* That is because, when Commercial Bank is quoting its Merchant Selling rate, it is based on the presumption that it will buy the USD at the interbank market selling rate.

   If the margin were to be deducted, the bank would pass on a lower rate to the importer and, thereby, recover less from the importer than it would be paying International Bank in the inter-bank market and incurring a loss in the transaction.

   The rule is, therefore, that when a bank like Commercial bank quotes merchant selling rate, it must add the profit margin.

b. *Why is the merchant rate (arrived at 90.7590) rounded up to 90.76 and not reduced to 90.75?*

   That is because, in order to protect its profit, the bank would like to take as much INR as possible from the importer.

   Consider the situation where the merchant rate is 90.75 versus 90.76.

   90.75 – Commercial Bank will recover INR 2,72,25,000– from the importer

   90.76 - Commercial Bank will recover INR 2,72,28,000– from the importer

Obviously, Commercial Bank would like to recover INR 2,72,28,000 from the importer rather than INR 2,72,25,000 and, hence, would quote the higher rate of 90.76.

c. The abovementioned flow for calculation of merchant selling rate is depicted in the following figure:

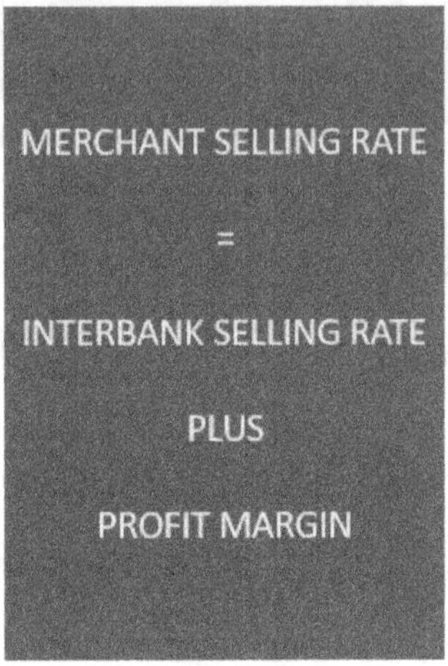

Figure 7.2 Calculation of merchant selling rate

Based on the above examples, Commercial Bank would quote 89.84 and 90.76 as its merchant buying rate and merchant selling rate, respectively, for USD INR.

These rates, with a little modification, are also used to arrive at the TT Buying rate and the TT Selling rate. The concept of TT rates and other types of exchange rates will be explained at in a later chapter.

[*Note: You have learnt that while quoting buying rate to merchant, the bank would like to pass on a lower rate so that it would part with lesser INR, thereby maximising its profit. Accordingly, merchant buying rate is ROUNDED DOWN.*

Hence, for example, if the merchant buying rate works out to 90.6784, it would be rounded down to 90.67 and not rounded off to the nearest paise, ie., 90.68.

Using the same logic of profit maximisation, while quoting selling rate to merchant, the bank would like to pass on a higher rate so that it would recover higher amount of INR from the customer.

Accordingly, merchant selling rate is ROUNDED UP. Hence, for example, if the merchant selling rate works out to 91.2535, it would be rounded up to 91.26 and not rounded off to the nearest paise, ie., 91.25.]

7.4 RATIONALE OF RETAINING EXCHANGE PROFIT MARGIN

You would have observed in this chapter that, in the process of buying and selling foreign currency in the interbank market - as a response to selling or buying foreign currency from the merchant (customer) - the bank always loads some amount of profit margin (or exchange margin).

What are the different factors, because of which the bank retains profit margin? These include the following:

- The forex market is volatile. Accordingly, in the time taken by the bank between carrying out the merchant transaction and covering the transaction in the interbank market, there is a time lag, during which the rates can move – sometimes quite significantly. This exposes the bank to foreign exchange risk.
- The above situation is further aggravated because banks do not cover each merchant transaction as they take place, but do the cover operations, in larger lots. This strategy naturally

builds in delay, during which time the interbank rates can move against the bank.

- There are costs in covering in the interbank markets. These include cost of brokerage and cost of maintaining a trading room for such operations.
- There are operational and administrative costs involved. These include staff costs, SWIFT costs, cost of regulatory and audit compliance, costs of IT systems, deal settlements and account reconciliation.
- There are counterparty risks – the possibility of failure of the bank in the interbank market - from whom funds are to be received.
- There is always the rationale of generating reasonable profit, after factoring in all related costs and manageable risks.

7.5 TYPES OF RATES QUOTED TO MERCHANTS

In this chapter, you have learnt how merchant rates are calculated.

There are different types of rates (within the overall umbrella of buying and selling rates) that banks quote to their customers.

These are TT buying rate, TT selling rate, bill buying rate and bill selling rate. These different types of rates are covered, in greater detail in a later chapter of the book.

Check Your Understanding

7.1 The ruling interbank USD INR rate is 90.2525 / 3500. Given that, as a matter of policy, Commercial Bank keeps 0.15% as profit margin, calculate the exchange rate that will be given by the Bank to Abacus Ltd, a company that wants to remit USD 25,000 to Hongkong towards freight charges?

In this example, Commercial Bank will require to SELL USD 25,000 to Abacus Ltd, by BUYING the same from the inter-bank market at the market selling rate. The merchant rate is calculated as follows:

Interbank USD INR rate	90.3500
ADD profit margin @ 0.15%	0.1355
	90.4855
Merchant USD INR Selling rate	**90.49**

Check Your Understanding

7.2 The ruling interbank USD INR rate is 90.2525 / 3500. Given that, as a matter of policy, Commercial Bank keeps 0.20% as profit margin, calculate the quote that will be given by the Bank to Mr Mehta, who has received a remittance of USD 5,000 from his son who works in Dubai?

In this example, Commercial Bank will have to BUY the USD 5,000 from Mr Mehta, and thereafter SELL the amount in the inter-bank market at the market buying rate. The merchant rate is computed as follows:

Interbank USD INR rate	90.2525
LESS profit margin @ 0.20%	0.1805
	90.0720
Merchant USD INR Buying rate	**90.07**

Check Your Understanding

7.3 Multi Corporation Ltd (MLC) required to remit USD 3,000,000 to their principals in Australia towards technology transfer fees. Given that the ruling interbank USD INR rate is 90.0050 / 1025, and keeping a profit margin of 5 paise, what is the INR amount required to be debited to the Company's cash credit account?

In this example, Commercial Bank will SELL USD 3,000,000 to Multi Corporation Ltd by buying the amount from the inter-bank market at the market SELLING rate.

The merchant rate and INR equivalent are calculated as follows:

Interbank USD INR rate	90.1025
ADD profit margin	0.0500
	90.1525
Merchant USD INR Selling rate	90.16
Amount to be debited to Co's account for selling it USD 3,000,000 @ 90.16	**INR 27,04,80,000**

EXERCISE 7

1. Gala Exports has received USD 32,000- as proceeds of shipment of pharmaceuticals to Uganda. They have requested their bankers, Commercial Bank, to credit the amount to their current account in INR.

   The ruling USD INR inter-bank rates are 90.3250/75.

   Given that Commercial Bank keeps exchange margin of 0.20%, what is the amount of INR that will be credited to the current account of the exporter?

2. Gala Exports had received USD 32,000- as proceeds of one its export consignments to Uganda. The buyer found some of the pharmaceuticals of inferior quality and have, therefore, filed a claim of USD 5,500- on the exporters.

   The exporters have requested their bank, Commercial Bank to remit the claim amount. Given that Commercial Bank keeps profit margin of Rs 0.10 per USD, what is the merchant rate that will be quoted for the remittance?

   The USD INR inter-bank rates prevailing are 90.3225/50.

3. Omega Industries requires to make an advance payment of USD 55,000- to their suppliers in Norway, for import of certain industrial instruments.

   Given that Commercial Bank keeps an exchange profit margin of 0.20%, what will be the merchant rate quoted to Omega?

   The prevailing interbank USD INR rates are 91.2225/50.

4. Due to a delay in shipment due to war conditions in West Asia, the suppliers in Norway have cancelled the order and refunded the amount of USD 55,000- to Omega Industries.

   Given prevailing inter-bank USD INR rates of 90.8800/25, and that Commercial Bank retains an exchange margin of 7.5 paise, what is the rate that will be quoted by the bank for handling the refund transaction?

Chapter 8

Cross Rates

8.1 THE WHAT AND WHY OF CROSS RATES

In the forex market in India, subject to relevant regulations, INR can be converted to many currencies like USD, EUR, GBP, JPY, CHF, HKD, SGD, AUD, and so on. However, in the interbank forex market in India, exchange rate is quoted only for the USD INR pair. Then, how would an exporter or an importer know the exchange rate for, say, EUR or GBP or JPY, etc.in equivalent INR?

The exchange rate of any foreign currency, other than USD, to INR has to be derived by arriving at the CROSS RATE.

A cross rate is an exchange rate between two currencies (for example EUR and INR) that are both valued against a common third currency. The USD is the currency that is frequently used in foreign currency exchange markets to establish the values of the pair being exchanged.

If the EUR INR rate has to be determined, it has to be done by first reckoning the EUR USD rate and then adjusting it with the USD INR rate. But why do we have to drag the USD in the picture in order to determine the EUR INR rate? That is because, in the

Indian forex interbank market, rate is available only for the USD INR pair.

In order to derive at the EUR INR rate therefore, one needs to also know what the prevailing EUR USD rate is, and then calculate the EUR INR rate.

Example:

USD INR rate	90.1000 / 90.2000
EUR USD rate	1.2100 / 1.2150
Calculating cross rate EUR INR	(90.1000 x 1.2100) / (90.2000 x 1.2150)
∴ EUR INR cross rate	109.0210 / 109.5930

In the above calculation, the following aspects may be noted:

a. USD INR rate is a *direct* quotation

b. EUR USD rate is an *indirect* quotation

c. Where conditions (a) and (b) both exist, cross rates can be obtained by multiplying the respective buying rates as also the respective selling rates.

d. In this example, therefore, the EUR INR cross rate is derived by multiplying the bid and offer USD INR rates with the corresponding bid and offer EUR USD rates, ie., 90.1000 x 1.2100 and 90.2000 x 1.2150.

e. As such, through the multiplication exercise, the EUR INR rates derived are 109.0210 and 109.5930.

f. According to the above calculations, the Bank can BUY 1 EUR for INR 109.0210 from the customer and the Bank can SELL 1 EUR for INR 109.5930, to the customer.

The above rule seems to be very simple – just multiply the corresponding rates to arrive at the cross rate.

This can be depicted, diagrammatically, as follows:

IF USD / INR = 90.10 / 20

X X

AND EUR / USD = 1.2100/2150

EUR / INR = (90.10 X 1.2100) / (90.20 X 1.2150)

= 109.0210 / 109.5930

Figure 8.1 EUR INR cross rate

But what is the rationale of the calculation? That needs to be understood.

8.2 CALCULATING EUR INR BUYING RATE

A bank will quote the EUR INR buying rate to its exporter customer, who has EUR to sell to the bank. Let us assume that Cosmos Exports has received export proceeds of EUR 200,000 and wants to convert the same into INR. It, therefore, approaches its bank, Commercial Bank for EUR INR buying rate.

What Commercial Bank will do to derive the EUR INR rate:

Commercial Bank will buy EUR 200,000 from its customer, Cosmos Exports. However, the Indian forex interbank market quotes only the USD INR rate. Hence, Commercial Bank has to first convert the EUR into USD, and thereafter convert the resultant USD into INR.

For converting the EUR into USD, Commercial Bank needs to obtain EUR USD quote from a bank in the overseas market, say, Multinational Bank (MNB). Let's say that the EUR USD rate quoted by MNB is 1.2100 / 1.2150.

Commercial Bank can SELL EUR 200,000 to MNB at its interbank BUYING rate @ 1.2100. Accordingly, Commercial Bank will sell EUR 200,000 to MNB @ 1.2100 and receive USD 242,000 (200,000 x 1.2100).

Now that Commercial Bank has USD 242,000, it can sell the USD and obtain INR in the Indian forex market - at the interbank USD buying rate.

The prevailing USD INR rate is 90.1000 / 90.2000. It will, therefore, sell USD 242,000 @ 90.1000 and receive INR 2,18,04,200 in exchange.

Hence, the EUR 200,000 = INR 2,18,04,200,

or 1 EUR = 2,18,04,200 ÷ 200,000

<u>= 109.0210</u> (which is the same as 90.10 x 1.2100).

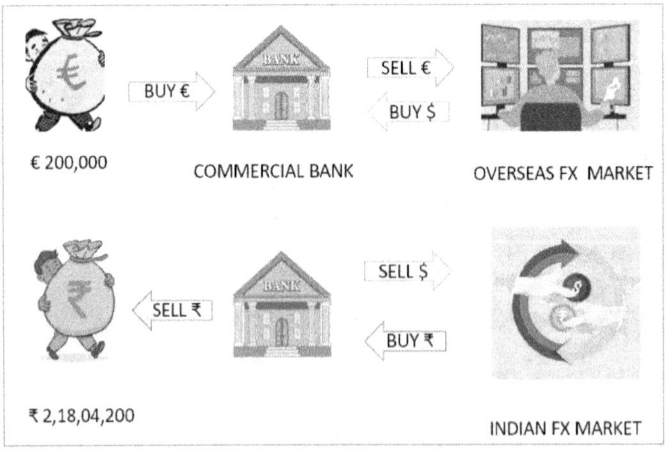

Figure 8.2 Mechanism for arriving at EUR INR buying rate

*The mechanism for calculating the cross rate, using intermediate foreign currencies, as seen in this example and other examples to follow, is known as the **Chain Rule**.*

8.3 CALCULATING EUR INR SELLING RATE

A bank will quote the EUR INR selling rate to its importer customer, who requires to buy EUR from the bank. For example, India Imports has to make payment of raw materials amounting to EUR 500,000 that it has imported from France, and, therefore, approaches its bank, Commercial Bank for EUR INR selling rate.

What Commercial Bank will do to derive the EUR INR rate:

Commercial Bank cannot buy EUR from the Indian forex market, as the Indian interbank market only provides quotes for USD INR. Hence, Commercial bank must use the INR provided by India Imports and BUY USD in the Indian market.

The prevailing EUR USD rate in the overseas market is 1.2100 / 1.2150.

Hence, a bank can buy EUR in the interbank market at the market's selling rate. The interbank EUR USD selling rate is 1.2150 and in order to buy EUR 500,000, an amount of USD 6,07,500 (500,000 x 1.2150) is required.

The prevailing USD INR rate is 90.1000 / 90.2000. Commercial Bank, will, therefore use INR made available to it by India Imports and buy USD 6,07,500 at the interbank selling rate, ie., 90.2000.

The amount of INR debited to India Imports' current account will be (6,07,500 x 90.2000) = INR 5,47,96,500.

Having converted INR into USD 607,500, Commercial Bank will now proceed to sell the USD 607,500 and buy EUR 500,000 @ 1.2150, which will be now available to its customer India Imports.

Hence, the EUR 500,000 = INR 5,47,96,500

or 1 EUR = 5,47,96,500 ÷ 500,000

= **109.5930** (which is the same as 90.20 x 1.2150).

Accordingly, Commercial Bank's EUR INR rate will be 109.0210 / 109.5930, or 109.02 / 109.60.

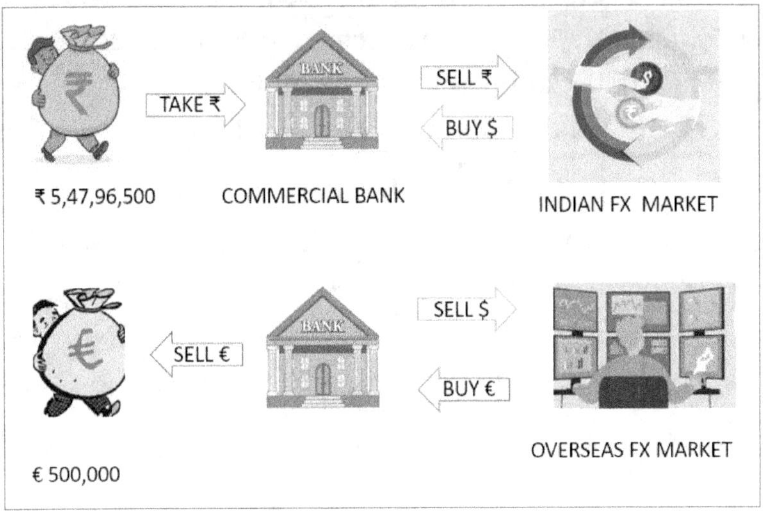

Figure 8.3 Mechanism for arriving at EUR INR selling rate

The formula given in this section can be applied in any Foreign Currency (FC) / INR quote, where the intermediate quote using USD is an ***indirect quote*** *(like the EUR USD quote).* Hence the multiplication formula can also be used for quotes like GBP INR, AUD INR, NZD INR, etc since in all these instances, their quote (GBP USD, AUD USD, NZD USD) are indirect quotes.

For example, if USD INR = 90.1800 / 90.2300

And GBP USD = 1.3310 / 1.3350, then

GBP INR = (90.1800 x 1.3310) / (90.2300 x 1.3350) = 120.0296 / 120.4570

However, the multiplication rule cannot be applied where the intermediate quote using USD is also a direct quote, like USD JPY and calculations involving INR quotes for such currencies, example, JPY INR are worked out in a different way, as per the examples that follow.

Check Your Understanding

8.1 Mr Sahani wants to buy a draft for EUR 10,000 for his son's education in Paris University. Given that the interbank EUR USD rate is 1.1025 / 1100 and USD INR rate is 90.1500 / 2000, what will be the EUR INR rate that will be quoted to Mr Sahani by Commercial Bank? Assume a profit margin at 0.20%.

In this example, Mr Sahani will require to BUY EUR 10,000 from Commercial Bank, who will sell the same at its merchant EUR INR selling rate, which is calculated as follows:

Applicable Interbank EUR USD rate	1.1100
Applicable Interbank USD INR rate	90.2000
EUR INR cross rate (using chain rule)	1.1100 x 90.2000
∴ EUR INR rate	100.122
ADD profit margin @ 0.20%	0.2002
	100.3222
Merchant EUR INR selling rate	**100.33**

Check Your Understanding

8.2 Godwin Exports has received export proceeds of GBP 75,000. Given that interbank rates for GBP USD is 1.3500 / 3600 and USD INR is 90.6500/ 7500, what will be rate quoted to the Company by Commercial Bank. Assume a profit margin at 0.15%.

In this example, Godwin Exports will require to SELL GBP 75,000 to Commercial Bank, who will buy the same at its merchant GBP INR buying rate, which is calculated as follows:

Applicable Interbank GBP USD rate	1.3500
Applicable Interbank USD INR rate	90.6500
GBP INR cross rate (using chain rule)	1.3500 x 90.6500
∴ GBP INR rate	122.3775
LESS profit margin @ 0.15%	0.1836
	122.1939
Merchant GBP INR buying rate	**122.39**

Check Your Understanding

8.3 Mr Shamsi had bought a forex travel card loaded with AUD 5,000 when he was going to visit Australia on a holiday. On returning to India, he had unspent balance of AUD 1,000 in the card.

The interbank rates ruling at that time are AUD USD 0.6500 / 6600 and USD INR 91.2500 / 3500.

What is the amount of INR that Commercial Bank will credit to Mr Shamsi's SB account assuming that the bank loads a profit margin of INR 0.50 and forex card cancellation charges of INR 250?

In this example, Mr Shamsi will require to SELL AUD 1,000 to Commercial Bank, who will buy the same at its merchant AUD INR selling rate. The exchange rate and amount of INR that will be credited to the customer's SB account is calculated as follows:

Applicable Interbank AUD USD rate	0.6500
Applicable Interbank USD INR rate	91.2500
AUD INR cross rate (using chain rule)	0.6500 x 91.2500
∴AUD INR rate	59.3125
LESS profit margin @ INR 0.50	0.5000
	59.8125
Merchant AUD INR rate	**59.81**
INR equivalent of AUD 1,000	INR 59,810
LESS Forex card cancellation charges	250
Net credit to SB account	**INR 59,560**

8.4 CALCULATING JPY INR BUYING RATE

You have already learnt that, in the Indian forex market, foreign exchange quote is available only for USD INR pair. If the exchange rate of INR has to be determined against any other currency, we have to follow the Chain Rule and arrive at the cross rate.

When the cross rate of INR against any foreign currency, which is quoted on direct basis in the international market (like JPY) is required, it is not a procedure of straight multiplication. It is a little different, as can be seen from the following table.

USD INR rate	90.10 / 90.20
USD JPY rate	140.00 / 142.00
Calculating cross rate JPY INR	(90.10 ÷ 142.00) / (90.20 ÷ 140.00)
Cross rate JPR INR	0.6345 / 0.6443 (for INR 1), or, 63.45 / 64.43 (for INR 100, as per convention *)

* The convention is to quote rate for JPY 100, instead of JPY 1, because the JPY is numerically a small currency.

In the above calculation, the following aspects may be noted:

a. USD INR rate is a direct quotation

b. USD JPY rate is **also a direct quotation**

c. Where conditions (a) and (b) both exist, the JPY INR cross rate is derived by **dividing** the USD INR rates by the corresponding USD JPY for the other type of operation (ie., the USD JPY rate selling rate for a JPY INR buy operation and the USD JPY buying rate for a JPY INR sell operation, ie., 90.10 ÷ 142.00 and 90.20 ÷ 140.00.

d. As such, through the division exercise, the JPY INR rates derived are 0.6345 and 0.6443.

e. However, since the JPY is, numerically, a small currency, its rate is not expressed as against 1 JPY. Instead, JPY's rate is expressed as against 100 JPY, ie., 100 times 0.6345 and 100 times 0.6443 - which work out to 63.45 and 64.43.

f. According to the above calculations, you can BUY 100 JPY for INR 63.45 and SELL 100 JPY for INR 64.43.

This can be, diagrammatically, depicted as follows:

IF USD / INR = 90.10 / 20

AND USD / JPY = 140.00 / 142.00

JPY / INR = (90.10 ÷ 142.00) / (90.20 ÷ 140.00)

= 0.6345 / 0.6443

OR, 100 JPY = INR 63.45/ 64.43

Figure 8.4 JPY INR cross rate

The rationale of the above calculations is explained by means of the following examples.

Calculating JPY INR Buying rate

Example: Advent Exports has received export proceeds of JPY 10,000,000 and wants to convert the same into INR and, therefore, approaches its bank, Commercial Bank for JPY INR buying rate.

A bank will quote the JPY INR buying rate to its exporter customer, who has JPY to sell to the bank.

What Commercial Bank will do to derive the JPY INR rate:

Commercial Bank will buy JPY 10,000,000 from its customer, Advent Exports. However, the Indian forex market quotes only the USD INR rate. Hence, Commercial Bank has to first convert the JPY received from the Exporter into USD, and thereafter convert the USD into INR.

For converting the JPY into USD, Commercial Bank needs to obtain USD JPY quote from a bank in the overseas market, say, Multinational Bank (MNB). Let's say that the USD JPY rate quoted by MNB is 140.00 / 142.00.

Commercial Bank can SELL JPY 10,000,000 to MNB and BUY equivalent USD from MNB at its interbank USD JPY rate. But which rate?

USD JPY = 140.00 / 142.00

The interpretation of the above quote is that if you have 1 USD, you can sell it in the inter-bank market and get 140 JPY. Or if you want to buy 1 USD in the inter-bank market, you require 142 JPY.

But here the situation is such that Commercial bank has JPY 10,000,000 and wants to buy the equivalent USD amount. Hence, the second of the two rates, ie., USD JPY = 142.00 will be applicable (and not USD JPY = 140.00).

By using USD JPY rate of 142.00, Commercial Bank will receive USD (10,000,000 ÷ 142.00) ie., USD 70,422.54.

Having converted JPY into USD, Commercial Bank can now proceed to sell the USD 70,422.54 in the Indian forex market at the prevailing USD INR rate and generate INR.

In the Indian market, International Bank is quoting USD INR at 90.10 / 90.20.

Commercial Bank can sell the USD 70,422.54 to International Bank at the latter's USD INR buying rate, ie., 90.10.

As such, Commercial Bank will receive:

70,422.54 x 90.10 = INR 63,45,070.85 from International Bank for credit to current account of Advent Exports.

From the above calculations, it is seen that:

1 USD = 142.00 JPY, and

1 USD = 90.10 INR

∴ 142.00 JPY = 90.10 INR,

or 100 JPY = (90.10 ÷ 142.00) x 100 = **63.45 INR**

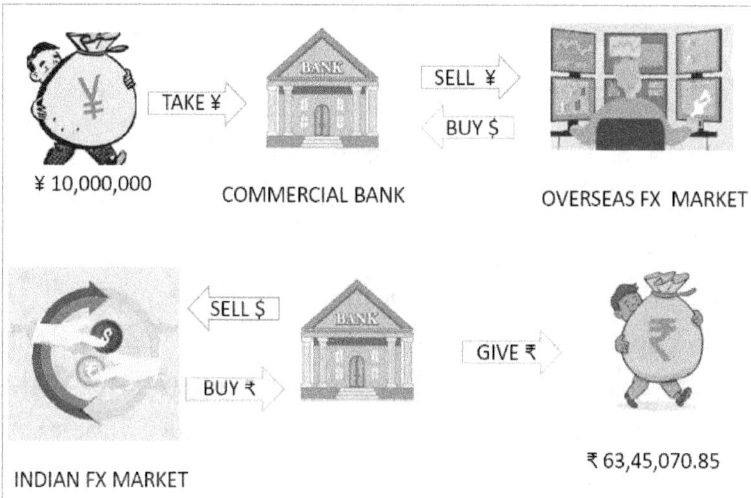

Figure 8.5 Mechanism for arriving at JPY INR buying rate

8.5 CALCULATING JPY INR SELLING RATE

Suresh Imports requires JPY 5,000,000 for making payment for a machinery imported from Japan and, therefore, approaches its bank, Commercial Bank for JPY INR selling rate.

A bank will quote the JPY INR selling rate to its importer customer, who has to buy JPY from the bank.

What Commercial Bank will do to derive the JPY INR rate:

Commercial Bank cannot buy JPY from the Indian forex market, as the Indian interbank market only provides quotes for

USD INR. Hence, Commercial bank must use the INR provided by Suresh Imports and BUY USD in the Indian market. But what amount of USD should be bought?

The prevailing USD JPY rate, which has been quoted by MNB in the overseas market, is 140.00 / 142.00.

Since MNB will give JPY to Commercial Bank and take USD from it, it will try and give the minimum amount of JPY. In this case, therefore, it will give 140.00 JPY for each USD (and not 142.00 JPY). Hence the applicable USD JPY rate will be 140.00.

By using USD JPY rate of 140.00, Commercial Bank will receive JPY 5,000,000 from MNB by selling it USD (5,000,000 ÷ 140.00) ie., USD 35,714.29.

Having calculated the amount of USD it must sell (USD 35,714.29) in order to buy JPY 5,000,000, Commercial Bank can now proceed to buy USD 35,714.29 in the Indian forex market at the prevailing USD INR rate against INR, which will be provided by Suresh Imports in its current account.

The prevailing USD INR rate is 90.10 / 90.20. Commercial Bank, will, therefore use INR to buy USD 35,714.29 at the interbank selling rate, ie., 90.20. The amount of INR so required and, therefore, debited to India Imports' current account will be (35,714.29 x 90.20) = INR 32,21,428.96.

From the above calculations, it is seen that:

1 USD = 140.00 JPY, and

I USD = 90.20 INR

Or, 140.00 JPY = 90.20 INR,

Or 100 JPY = (90.20 ÷ 140.00) x 100 = **64.43 INR**

Accordingly, Commercial Bank's JPY INR rate will be 63.45 / 64.43. (Quoted for 100 JPY)

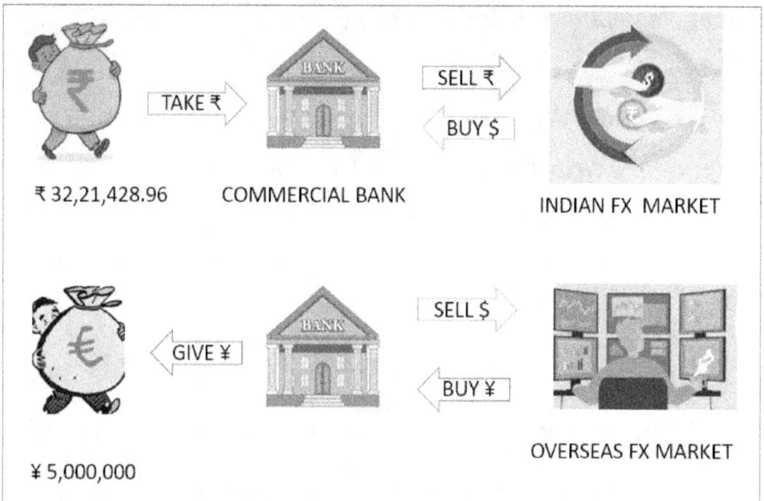

Figure 8.6 Mechanism for arriving at JPY INR selling rate

The formula given in this section can be applied in any Foreign Currency (FC) INR quote, *where the intermediate rate using USD is also a **direct** quote.*

Hence, the formula can be used for calculating cross rates for currency pairs like JPY INR, CHF INR, CAD INR, HKD INR, etc., since in all these cases, the quote for the intermediary transaction, viz., (USD JPY, USD CHF, USD CAD, USD HKD) are direct quotes.

For example, if USD INR = 91.18 / 91.23

And USD HKD = 7.83 / 7.88, then

HKD INR = (91.18 ÷ 7.88) / (91.23 ÷ 7.83) = 11.5711/ 11.6513.

[Note: You will have observed that whilst most in most exchange rate quotations, the currencies are expressed in single units, for example, 1 USD, 1 EUR, 1 GBP, 1 CAD, etc., there are some currencies, which because of their low unit value, are expressed in larger units, like 100 JPY.

Some currencies, other than JPY which are expressed in larger units include Indonesian Rupiah (1000 or 10000 IDR), Vietnamese Dong (1000 or 10000 VND) and South Korean Won (100 or 1000 KRW). Such expressions are based on market practice and local bank customs.]

Check Your Understanding

8.4 Border Exports has received export proceeds of SGD 200,000.

Given that interbank rates for USD SGD is 1.3200 / 3300 and USD INR is 90.1500/ 2000, what will be rate quoted to the Company by Commercial Bank?

(Assume profit margin at 0.20%.)

In this example, Border Exports will require to SELL SGD 200,000 to Commercial Bank, who will buy the same at its merchant SGD INR BUYING rate, which is calculated as follows:

Interbank USD SGD rate	1.3200 / 1.3300
Applicable Interbank USD INR rate	90.1500
GBP INR cross rate (using chain rule)	90.15 ÷ 1.3300
∴ SGD INR rate	67.7820
LESS profit margin @ 0.20%	0.1356
	67.6464
Merchant SGD INR buying rate	**67.64**

Check Your Understanding

8.5 Mr Sen wants to send a remittance for AED 500 towards a one year's subscription for a technical magazine which is published from Dubai.

Given that the interbank USD AED rate is 3.6700 / 6900 and USD INR rate is 90.9500 / 90.0500, what will be the AED INR rate that will be quoted to Mr Sen by Commercial Bank?

(Assume volatility cushion a profit margin at INR 0.50.)

In this example, Mr Sen will require to buy AED 500 from Commercial Bank, who will sell the same at its merchant AED INR SELLING rate, which is calculated as follows:

Interbank USD AED rate	3.6700 / 3.6800
Applicable Interbank USD INR rate	90.0500
AED INR cross rate (using chain rule)	90.0500 ÷ 3.6700
∴ AED INR rate	24.5368
ADD profit margin of 50 paise	0.5000
	25.0368
Merchant AED INR selling rate	**25.04**

Check Your Understanding

8.6 Continental Imports has purchased an electronic microscope from Sweden at a cost of SEK 1,000,000 and requires to make the payment to the supplier.

Given that the interbank USD SEK rate is 9.6900 / 7100 and USD INR rate is 91.3500 / 3800, what will be the SEK INR rate that will be quoted to the Company by Commercial Bank, and what will be the amount in INR required to be paid by the Company?

(Assume profit margin at 10 paise)

In this example, Continental Imports will require to buy SEK 1,000,000 from Commercial Bank, who will sell the same at its merchant SEK INR SELLING rate, which is calculated as follows:

Interbank USD SEK rate	9.6900/ 7100
Applicable Interbank USD INR rate	91.3800
SEK INR cross rate (using chain rule)	91.3800 ÷ 9.69
∴ SEK INR rate	9.4303
ADD profit margin of 50 paise	0.5000
	9.9303
Merchant SEK INR rate	9.94
INR to be recovered for SEK 1,000,000	**INR 99,40,000**

8.6 WHAT IS A PIP?

A pip is a term that is often used in foreign exchange quotations. The full form of "pip" is *"Percentage in Point"*.

In interbank markets, foreign exchange rates are normally quoted up to 4 places of decimal. For example,

EUR USD = 1.1550 / 1.1560

GBP USD = 1.3675 / 1.3685

USD INR = 91.2175 / 91.2200

The pip is the 4th decimal place in the quote (1/10,000) and this is underlined in the above quotes. It means that if you say the EUR USD has moved by 5 pips, it would have moved from, say, 1.1550 to 1.1555.

While this is the convention for pip in almost all currency pairs, the quotes involving JPY are an exception. For JPY quotes, a pip is 1/100th, as against 1/10,000th for other pairs. In rates involving JPY, the quotes are only up to the 2nd place of decimal.

For example,

USD JPY = 140.24 / 140.28

EUR JPY = 162.74 / 162.82

The pips for the above quotes are underlined.

Sometimes, in interbank markets, for certain currency pairs which are popular, such as EUR USD or GBP USD, quotes are even given for up to **the fifth decimal place:**

For example, EUR USD = 1.15505 / 1.15605

Or, GBP USD = 1.36755 / 1.36855

In such quotes, the 5th decimal is known as a *pipette.*

The use of pipettes is rare, and occur for those currency pairs whose markets are very active, with very large volumes of transactions.

8.7 CERTAIN CONVENTIONS IN THE INDIAN FOREX MARKET

- Interbank rates are quoted up to 4 decimal places. For example, USD INR = 91.0225.
- In USD INR quotes, the last two decimal places for interbank quotes are in multiples of '25'. For example, 91.0200 or 91.0225 or 91.0250 or 91.0275. Not, say, 91.0218 or 91.0233.
- Merchant rates that are quoted to customers are up to 2 decimal places only. For example, USD INR = 91.00 or 91.22 or 91.31. EUR INR = 109.66 or 109.32, etc.

[Note: in the case certain selected large customers, banks do quote the USD INR exchange rates up to 4 decimal places, with the last two places being in multiples of '25'. For example, 91.2225, 90.8450, 90.2100, etc.]

- Customer transactions are rounded off to the nearest whole Rupee.

  For example, USD 29,642.34 @ USD INR 91.11 will be INR 27,00,714- and not INR 27,00,713.59.

Check Your Understanding

8.7 If the EUR USD rate is quoted at 1.2365, and the rate moves up by 6 pips, what will be the new rate?

a. 1.2359

b. 1.2965

c. 1.2425

d. 1.2371

Answer: d

Check Your Understanding

8.8 If the GBP JPY rate is quoted at 190.36 and the rate moves down by 2 pips, what will be the new rate?

a. 188.36

b. 190.16

c. 190.34

d. 190.38

Answer: c

EXERCISE 8

1. Given the following exchange rates, calculate the NZD INR buying cross rate:

   USD INR = 91.1025 / 1075

   NZD USD = 0.5811 / 15

2. Given the following exchange rates, calculate the CAD INR selling cross rate:

   USD INR = 90.9950 / 91.0000

   USD CAD = 1.3722 / 24

3. Given the following exchange rates, calculate the IDR INR buying and selling cross rates:

   USD INR = 90.5550 / 75

   USD IDR = 16979 / 17256

4. Action Exports has received proceeds of an export bill amounting to SGD 312,000. Given the following prevailing exchange rates, derive the applicable SGD INR rate, assuming that the bank retains exchange profit margin of 0.10%.

   Prevailing exchange rates are:

   USD INR 90.6250 / 75

   USD SGD 1.2822 / 26

5. Glory Steels Ltd imports coal from Australia and is required to make an advance remittance of AUD 1,250,000.

   Given the following exchange rates, calculate the appropriate AUD INR cross rate.

   USD INR 91.2175 / 2200

   AUD USD 0.7101 / 03

6. Chemsel Exports Ltd has received export proceeds amounting to USD 5,250,333-. Looking at the large amount of remittance, it has asked its bankers for a fine rate and has been quoted USD INR rate of 91.2175.

   Based on the given exchange rate, what is the amount that the bank will credit the Company's current account?

Chapter 9

Types of Foreign Currency Accounts

9.1 NOSTRO ACCOUNTS

The concept of nostro, vostro and loro accounts is integral to any study of foreign exchange.

Let us consider that Commercial Bank has bought EUR 500,000 against USD from Multi National Bank (MNB) at EUR USD rate of 1.1435. This means that Commercial Bank will RECEIVE EUR 500,000 from MNB against PAYMENT of USD (500,000 x 1.1435), ie., USD 571,750.

To make payment of USD 571,750 to MNB, Commercial Bank must know where MNB is maintaining its USD account. Let us say that MNB has a USD account with Citibank, New York.

Moreover, having bought EUR 500,000, Commercial Bank must have a EUR account in which MNB can remit the EUR amount. Let us say that Commercial Bank has a EUR account with Deutsche Bank, Frankfurt.

Hence, all banks that undertake foreign exchange transactions, must maintain accounts in those foreign currencies in which they transact.

These foreign currency accounts are called *Nostro accounts* (Our account with you). Hence, the USD account of MNB with Citibank, NY, is MNB's USD nostro account, and Commercial Bank's EUR account with Deutsche Bank is Commercial Bank's EUR nostro account.

Nostro accounts are, therefore, "our account with you".

MNB will communicate to Commercial Bank "Please credit USD 571,750 to our nostro account with Citibank, NY" and Commercial Bank will communicate to MNB "Please credit EUR 500,000 to our nostro account with Deutsche Bank, Frankfurt".

9.2 VOSTRO ACCOUNTS

On the contrary, Vostro account means "your account with us". Hence, in this example, for Citibank NY, MNB's USD account is its vostro account with Citibank. It will address MNB's USD account as "your USD vostro account with us". And Deutsche Bank will address Commercial Bank's EUR account as "your EUR vostro account with us".

The concepts of nostro and vostro accounts are depicted, diagrammatically, as follows:

Figure 9.1 Nostro and Vostro Accounts

9.3 LORO ACCOUNTS

The third type of terminology of accounts, which is used in foreign exchange transactions – though much less than nostro and vostro – arc Loro accounts.

The term Loro account is used when a third bank refers to the nostro account of another bank. For example, you have seen that Multi National Bank maintains its USD nostro account with Citibank, NY. If a third bank like, say, Society Bank requires to refer to that account, it will term it as Multi National Bank's Loro account with Citibank, NY.

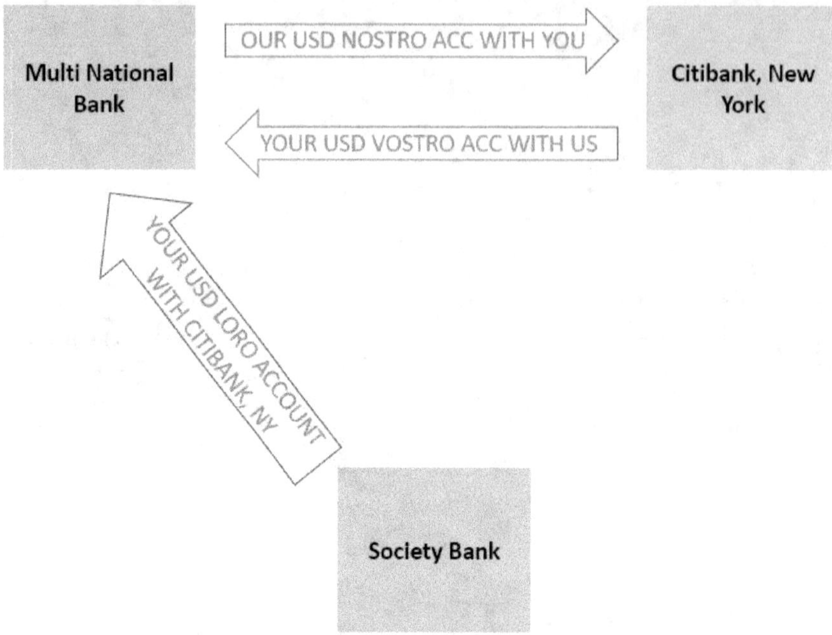

Figure 9.2 Loro Accounts

Therefore, summing up,

NOSTRO ACCOUNT = OUR ACCOUNT WITH YOU

VOSTRO ACCOUNT = YOUR ACCOUNT WITH US

LORO ACCOUNT = YOUR ACCOUNT WITH THEM

[Note: Nostro, vostro and loro are Italian words and mean "our", "your" and "their", respectively.]

EXERCISE 9

1. Citibank New York maintains an INR account with State Bank of India, Mumbai.

   For Citibank, NY, the account in question is its:

   a. INR nostro account

   b. USD nostro account

   c. INR vostro account

   d. USD vostro account

2. Bank of India, Mumbai, maintains a EUR account with its own Paris branch.

   For Bank of India, Mumbai, the account in question is its:

   a. INR nostro account

   b. EUR nostro account

   c. INR vostro account

   d. EUR vostro account

3. Citibank New York maintains an INR account with State Bank of India. For JP Morgan Bank, London, this account will be referred as what type of account in the name of Citibank, NY?

   a. Nostro account

   b. Vostro account

   c. Loro account

4. Alpha Bank has sold USD against INR from Beta Bank. In order to settle the transaction, what information will be required by Alpha Bank, with respect to Beta Bank?

   a. Their INR nostro account

   b. Their USD vostro account

   c. Their USD loro account

   d. Their USD nostro account

5. Gamma Bank has bought EUR against USD from Delta Bank. In order to settle the transaction, what information will be required by Gamma Bank, with respect to Delta Bank?

   a. Their USD nostro account

   b. Their EUR nostro account

   c. Their USD vostro account

   d. Their EUR vostro account

6. Gamma Bank has sold EUR against USD from Delta Bank. In order to settle the transaction, what information will be required by Gamma Bank, with respect to Delta Bank?

   a. Their USD nostro account

   b. Their EUR nostro account

   c. Their USD vostro account

   d. Their EUR vostro account

Chapter 10

Value Dates in Foreign Exchange Transactions

10.1 WHAT IS A VALUE DATE?

We are very familiar with foreign exchange rates as they are quoted. For example, let us suppose that today, say, 10th March 2026, rates quoted are:

USD INR = 91.5050 / 75

USD JPY = 155 / 157

EUR USD = 1.1611 / 41, etc, etc.

The question then arises "*Are these rates for exchanging currency today, or tomorrow, or some other day? What is the value date for these rates?*"

A *Value Date* is the date when the exchange of the currencies in the pair actually take place – irrespective of the date on which the transaction happened.

10.2 DIFFERENT TYPES OF VALUE DATES

There are, basically two types of time frames when the exchange of currencies take place – those in the short term (ie., from today to two business days ahead) and those in the longer term (ie., those where the exchange of currencies take place on a date which is more than two business days ahead from the transaction date).

In the short term, the exchange (or, settlement) of the currencies can take place, either:

- today (ie., transaction date), or
- one business day forward (ie., transaction date + 1 business day), or
- two business days forward (ie., transaction date + 2 business days).

These value dates are known, in foreign exchange jargon, as ***CASH, TOM AND SPOT***, respectively.

[Note: Value date Cash is also known as Ready.]

Any value date which lies beyond the spot date (ie., transaction date + greater than 2 business days) is called a **FORWARD**. Depending upon the duration of the forward period, forex rates can be 15 days forward, 1 month forward, 6 months forward, or even 1 year forward.

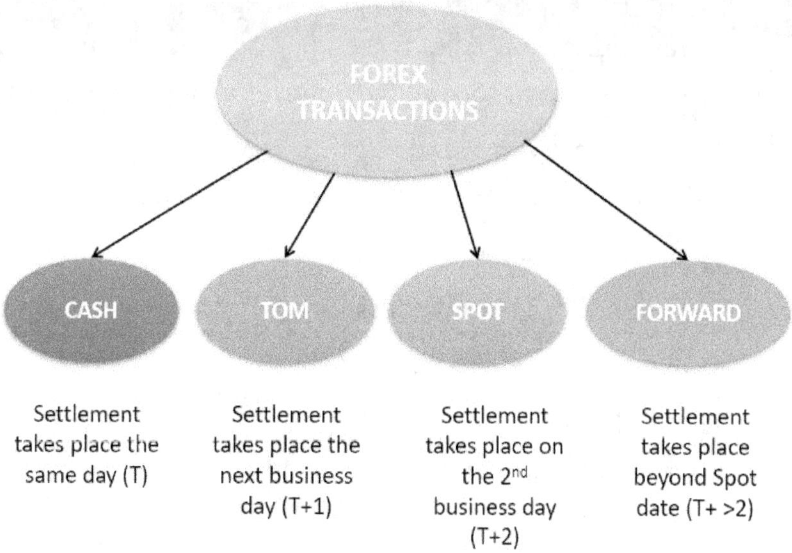

Figure 10.1 Value dates in foreign exchange transactions

It is also to be noted that, for any type of transaction (cash / tom / spot / forward) both centres of the currencies involved, must be open for foreign exchange business on the settlement (value) date.

[Note: To calculate the value date of a forward transaction, first the spot date is arrived at. To that date, the forward period is added.]

For example, for one-month forward rate,

Transaction date: 7th January 2026 (Wednesday)

Spot date: 9th January 2026

Value date for one-month forward transaction: 7th February 2026.

Check Your Understanding:

10.1 A forex transaction takes place on Tuesday, 4th June, 2024. What are the cash, tom, spot and 1-month forward value dates for that transaction date?

The dates are as follows:

Cash date – 4/6/2024 (Tuesday)

Tom date – 5/6/2024 (Wednesday)

Spot date – 6/6/2024 (Thursday)

One month forward – 5/7/2024 (Monday, since 4/7/2024 is a Sunday, and hence not a business day)

Check Your Understanding

10.2 A forex transaction takes place on Friday, 7th June, 2024. What are the cash, tom, spot and 1-month forward rates for that date?

The dates are as follows:

Cash date – 7/6/2024 (Friday)

Tom date – 10/6/2024 (Monday, as 8/6/2024 and 9/6/2024 are Saturday and Sunday, and hence not business days)

Spot date – 11/6/2024 (Tuesday)

One month forward – 7/7/2024

Therefore, coming back to question,

"*Whether the forex rates which are commonly quoted are for exchanging currency today, or tomorrow, or some other day? What is the value date for such rates?*",

The answer is that foreign exchange rates are customarily quoted for spot date, unless specified otherwise.

Hence, if we say that today's USD INR rate is 91.5050 / 75, it means that with the transaction being done today, say, 10th March 2026, the USD will be paid / received on spot date, which is 12th March 2026 and the INR will also be received / paid on the spot date 12th March 2026.

Hence, all forex rates are, customarily, quoted on spot basis, unless otherwise specified.

But then, why are forex rates commonly quoted of spot basis and not for settlement on the transaction date? The reasons are two-fold, viz.,

a. Banks entering into forex transactions need time to process the transactions, and

b. There can be time zone differences, too.

   Hence, if JPY is bought at a USD JPY rate of 151 on 10/3/2026, the JPY funds will be received at 10 am Tokyo time on 12/3/2026, whereas the USD funds will be paid at 10 am New York time on 12/3/2026, which 13 hours after the JPY leg is completed (the time difference between Tokyo and New York being 13 hours).

[Note: what is the difference between business day and working day?

*In foreign exchange, **business days** are typically Monday to Friday, excluding bank holidays, when financial markets and banks settle transactions.*

*On the other hand, **working days** are more flexible, often referring to any day an employee is scheduled to work, though not necessarily for foreign exchange transactions and which can include weekends or holidays,*

Therefore, for example, in India, Saturdays other than 2nd and 4th Saturdays are working days and banks handle routine transactions. However, forex markets are closed and, hence, on those Saturdays, though working days for the bank, are not considered as business days from foreign exchange point of view.]

EXERCISE 10

1. Alpha Bank bought USD 1,000,000- against INR on Monday, 23/2/2026 value spot. What will be the value date of the transaction?

   a. Monday, 23/2/2026

   b. Tuesday, 24/2/2026

   c. Wednesday, 25/2/2026

2. Beta Bank sold EUR 250,000- against USD on Wednesday, 24/12/2025 value spot. If banks are closed on 25th December for Christmas, what will be the value date for the transaction?

   a. Friday, 26/12/2025

   b. Saturday, 27/12/2025

   c. Monday, 29/12/2025

3. Gamma Bank sold INR 3 crores against USD, value cash on Tuesday, 17th March 2026. What will be the value date of the transaction, Thursday, 19/3/2026 being a public holiday?

   a. Tuesday, 17/3/2026

   b. Wednesday, 18/3/2026

   c. Friday, 20/3/2026

4. On 17/3/2026, Delta Bank bought JPY 50,000,000 against USD with value date 14/4/2026. What type of forex deal will that be, from value date point of view?

   a. Cash

   b. Spot

   c. Forward

5. Coastal Bank entered into a foreign exchange deal for buying USD 1,000,000 against EUR, value tom, on Friday 6/3/2026. What will be the value date of the deal?

   a. Friday, 6/3/2026

   b. Saturday, 7/3/2026

   c. Monday, 9/3/2026

   d. Tuesday, 10/3/2026

Chapter 11

Forward Rates and Forward Margins

11.1 WHAT ARE FORWARD RATES?

You have just learnt that forex rates can be quoted for settlement on short term basis (cash / tom / spot) or long-term basis (forward) and that, unless specified otherwise, forex rates are always quoted on spot basis.

In this Chapter, let us examine different aspects of forward rates.

Let us suppose that the USD INR spot rate on 1/1/2025 is 90.00. Will the forward rate for USD against INR, say for one month from today be the same? That is, 90.00? Or will the rate be something less (say, 89.50) or something (say, 90.50)? The answer is, that, it could be either of the two.

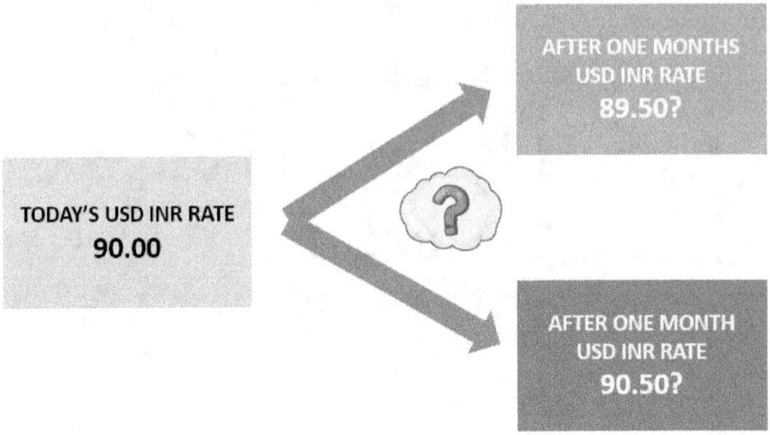

Figure 11.1 Uncertainty in future rates

This means that the forward rate is not the same as the spot rate. The USD INR rate, one month forward, can either be more than 90.00 or it can be less than 90.00.

If the forward USD INR rate is more than the spot rate, say 90.50, it denotes that the USD is at a **premium** against the INR. However, if the USD INR rate is less than the spot rate, say 89.50, it denotes that the USD is at a **discount** against the INR.

Hence, consider the following scenario:

Spot USD INR rate = 90.00

One month forward USD INR rate = 90.50

Conclusion: USD is at a premium against the INR. *This also automatically means that the INR is at a discount against the USD.*

and,

Spot USD INR rate = 90.00

One month forward USD INR rate = 89.50

Conclusion: USD is at a discount against the INR. *This also automatically means that the INR is at a premium against the USD.*

However, when one of the currencies is the home currency (in this case, INR), the premium or discount is always stated with respect to the foreign currency (in this case, USD).

Therefore, with USD INR spot rate being 90.00 and the one month forward rate being 90.50, we will normally always say that the USD is at a premium against the INR, instead of saying that the INR is at a discount against the USD (although both actually mean the same).

The difference between the spot and forward rates (in this case 90.50 – 90.00) is called the **forward margin**. Forward margins are also known as **swap points**.

When the currency is at a premium, the forward margin will be positive and where the currency is at a discount, the forward margin will be negative.

Example:

Spot USD INR = 90.00

One month forward USD INR = 90.50

Forward margin (premium) = (90.50 – 90.00) = + 0.50

Spot USD INR = 90.00

One month forward USD INR = 89.50

Forward margin (discount) = (89.50 – 90.00) = - 0.50

11.2 WHY ARE FORWARD RATES DIFFERENT FROM SPOT RATES?

There are a number of reasons which cause the forward rate to differ from the spot rate. However, the primary reason for the differing is because of the difference in the rates of interest prevailing in the two countries whose exchange rates are being compared.

In the case of USD INR, the forward rate differs from the spot rate because of the difference in the interest rate prevailing in USA and that prevailing in India. Because of the interest rate differential, there is a possibility of making risk-free arbitrage profit which, thereby, adjusts the forward exchange rate with relation to the spot rate in order that the arbitrage opportunity no longer exists.

The above phenomenon is explained by the Interest Rate Parity (IRP) Theorem, which is explained below.

Interest Rate Parity (IRP) Theorem

The Interest Rate Parity (IRP) is a theory regarding the relationship between the spot exchange rates and the forward exchange rates of two currencies, based on the prevailing interest rates.

The theory proves that if the spot rate and the forward rate are the same, then there is a possibility of making risk-free arbitrage profit. The forward rate, therefore, adjusts up or down, so as to eliminate such risk-free profits.

Under the IRP theory, one can borrow money in one country (say, USA) and place it as a deposit in another country, (say India) for a period of time (say, one year), resulting in profit because of the differences in the interest rates prevailing in the two countries.

Let us illustrate the aforesaid phenomenon by a figure:

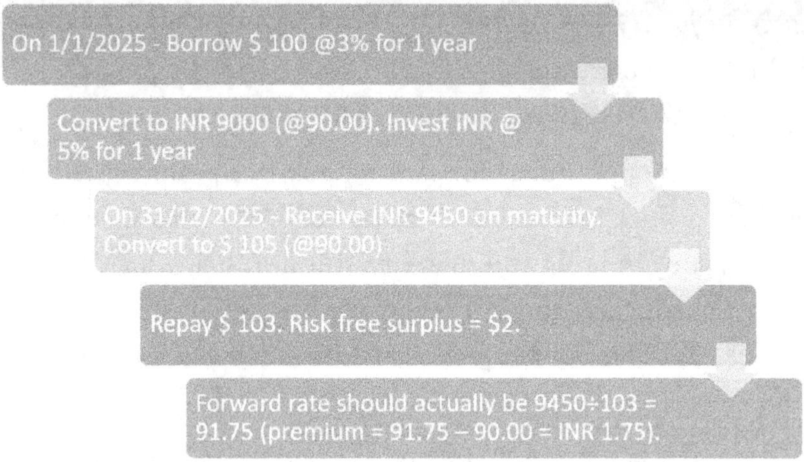

Figure 11.2 Interest Rate Parity Theory

Let us presume that the interest rates prevailing in USA and India are 3% and 5% p.a., respectively.

On 1/1/2025, a person borrows USD 100 for 1 year at the interest rate of 3% p.a. He then converts it into INR at the prevailing USD INR spot rate of 90.00.

He, therefore, receives INR 9,000- which he invests for 1 year in India, where the interest rate is 5% p.a.

On 31/12/2025, the date when both the USD loan and INR investment mature, he receives INR 9,450 (@ 5% p.a.).

Presuming that the spot exchange rate *has remained unchanged*, he converts INR 9,450 at the same exchange rate of 90.00 and receives USD 105.

The person then uses the amount of USD 105 to repay his loan (USD 100 + interest USD 3 = total USD 103) and he has, still, a surplus of USD 2 with him. This is the amount of risk-free profit.

[Note: Since the amounts used in the example was small, the amount of risk-free profit looks small (USD 2). Suppose, the transaction was for USD 10 million, instead of USD 100, the risk-free profit at the end of the year would have been USD 200,000!]

If such an opportunity for earning risk-free profit existed, there would be a huge increase in demand for USD (many people will like to borrow in USD and then invest it in INR), which will drive up the exchange rate for USD till it reaches (9,450 ÷ 103) = 91.75, which is, nothing but the one year forward exchange rate for the USD.

With spot rate being 90.00 and the one-year forward rate being 91.75, the premium on USD, against INR, works out to (91.75 – 90.00) = INR 1.75.

In addition to the Interest Rate Parity Theory, there are two other reasons which can cause forward rates to differ from their respective spot rates.

- These are Exchange and Capital Controls, and
- Demand and Supply of the respective Foreign Currencies.

As has been discussed so far, the forward rates differ from the spot rates because of the interest rate differentials. The IRP theory, however, presumes that there are no exchange or capital controls in the two countries involved (in our example, USA and India). The fact is, however, some extent of such controls almost always exist and there are very few countries in the world which are totally free of exchange and capital controls.

Imposition of exchange and capital controls by a country can impede the free international flow of funds and such impediments can, thereby, influence the forward rate causing a deviation from the forward rate that is calculated using the IRP Theory.

Another factor that can influence forward rates is the relative or demand supply of the involved currencies, in future. Hence, given the interest rate differentials between USA and India, it can normally be expected that the USD will quote at a premium to the INR.

Moreover, there could be an anticipated future event, for example, an expected large inflow of USD into India for a strategic investment, which will increase the supply of USD in the future. The increased future supply will have a weakening pressure on the USD (excess supply = decrease in price) and, under such circumstances, the USD may even be quoted at a discount to the INR for a particular time period, although the interest differentials between USA and India still remain.

Summing up, the factors influencing forward rates can be depicted as per the following figure.

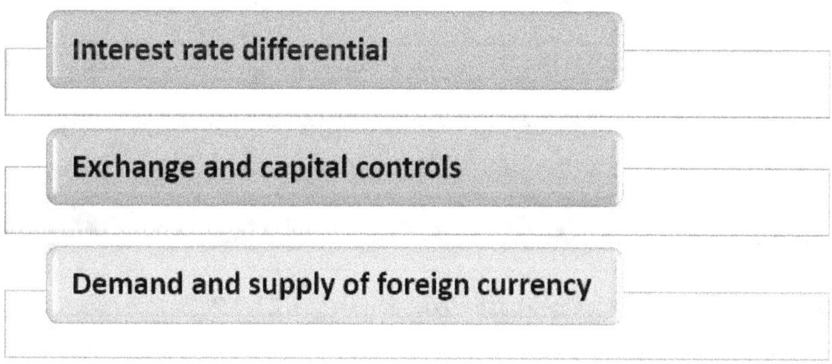

Figure 11.3 Factors Influencing Forward Rates

11.3 HOW TO DERIVE FORWARD RATES FROM SPOT RATES

Rule 11.1 – When a currency is at a premium, its forward margins are displayed in ascending order.

Example 1

Spot USD INR = 90.00

Forward margins:

July 20/21

Aug 34/35

Sep 51/52

Since the forward margins are in ascending order, it indicates that USD is at premium to INR.

Example 2

Spot USD INR = 90.00

Forward margins:

July 21/20

Aug 35/34

Sep 52/51

Since the forward margins are in descending order, it indicates that USD is at discount to INR.

Rule 11.2 – When a currency is quoted at a premium to another currency, the forward margin is ADDED to the spot rate in order to arrive at the forward rate.

Rule 11.3 – When a currency is quoted at a discount to another currency, the forward margin is SUBTRACTED from the spot rate in order to arrive at the forward rate.

Check Your Understanding

11.1 Let us presume that:

Spot USD INR = 90.42 / 43

Forward margin:

July = 7.00 / 9.00

August = 55.00 / 57.00

September = 102.00 / 103.00

October = 151.00 / 153.00

(Note: Market convention is to quote USD INR forward margins in terms of paise (ie., the margin for July is 7 paise / 9 paise)

Calculate the forward rates from July to October.

Since the forward margins are in ascending order, it means that USD is at premium to INR (Rule 11.1).

Hence, forward margin has to be added to spot rate to arrive at the forward rate (Rule 11.2). The forward rates will be as follow:

July USD INR = 90.49 / 52

August USD INR = 90.97 / 91.00

September USD INR = 91.44 / 46

October USD INR = 91.93 / 96

Check Your Understanding

11.2 Let us presume that:

Spot USD JPY = 146.85 / 95

Forward margin:

July = 2.00 / 1.00

August = 3.00 / 2.00

September = 4.00 / 3.00

Calculate the forward rates from July to September.

Since the forward margins are in descending order, it means that USD is at discount to JPY (Rule 11.1).

Hence, forward margin has to be subtracted from spot rate to arrive at the forward rate (Rule 11.3).

The forward rates will be as follow:

July USD JPY = 144.85 / 145.95

August USD JPY = 143.85 / 144.95

September USD JPY = 142.85 / 143.95

11.4 WHY IS DISCOUNT QUOTED / WRITTEN IN DESCENDING MANNER?

As has stated in this chapter, premium is quoted in an ascending order, whilst discount is quoted in a descending order.

A question which can arise here, is that why is that so? Why can discount not be quoted in an ascending order, similar to premium?

This can be explained as follows:

When a currency is quoted at a discount, its forward rate is lower than its spot rate.

Let us take the case of USD JPY, where USD is at a discount to JPY.

Illustrative rates are as follows:

USD JPY Spot 144.60 / 145.60

Forward margins:

1 month 2.00 / 1.00

2 months 4.00 / 2.00

3 months 5.00 / 4.00

The question is that, when the currency is at a discount, why are the forward margins written in descending order (2.00/1.00, 4.00/2.00, 5.00/4.00) and not in ascending order like premium (say, 1.00/2.00, 2.00/4.00, 4.00/5.00).

To understand this, the following points need to be noted:

a. The forward rate will always be less than the spot rate,

b. The resultant forward bid rate must always be less than the forward offer rate, and

c. There has to be a spread between the bid and offer margins for any forward time period.

Accordingly, if the forward margins, for a currency in discount were to be written in an ascending order, it is possible that on subtracting the discount from the spot rate (in order to arrive at the forward rate), the bid rate may become HIGHER than, or EQUAL TO the offer rate, Such a situation is not acceptable in any forex quote as it is anomalous and gives rise to an arbitrage opportunity.

Hence, writing the above forward margins is a descending order, the forward rates will be:

1 month 142.60 /144. 60

2 months 140.60 / 143.60

3 months 139.60 / 141.60

If, however, for sake of discussion, we write the forward margins in an *ascending order*, the forward rates (after deducting the forward margins) would be as follows:

USD JPY Spot 144.60 / 145.60

Forward margins:

1 month 1.00 / 2.00

2 months 2.00 / 4.00

3 months 4.00 / 5.00

USD JPY forward rates, after deducting the forward margins:

1 month 143.60 / 143.60

2 months 142.60 / 141.60

3 months 140.60 / 140.60

These rates are not tenable, because while in 1- and 3-months buckets, the bid and offer rates are identical and without any spread, in the 2-months bucket, the bid rate is actually more than the offer rate.

EXERCISE 11

1. The interbank USD INR rates and forward margins are as follows:

   Spot 90.2550 / 75

   Spot / 1 month 12 / 15

   Spot / 3months 34 / 35

   Spot / 6 months 82 / 85

   Under the circumstances, is USD ruling at a premium or at a discount against the INR?

   a. Premium

   b. Discount

2. The interbank EUR USD rates and swap points are as follows:

   Spot 1.1833 / 35

   Spot / 1 month 0.1719 / 0.1729

   Spot / 2 months 0.3365 / 0.3389

   Spot / 3 months 0.5622 / 0.5632

   Under the circumstances, is USD ruling at a premium or at a discount against the EUR?

   a. Premium

   b. Discount

3. The interbank USD INR rates and forward margins are as follows:

   Spot 90.2550 / 75

   Spot / 1 month 12 / 15

   Spot / 3months 34 / 35

   Spot / 6 months 82 / 85

   Under the circumstances, is INR ruling at a premium or at a discount against the USD?

   a. Premium

   b. Discount

4. The interbank EUR USD rates and swap points are as follows:

   Spot 1.1833 / 35

   Spot / 1 month 0.1719 / 0.1729

   Spot / 2 months 0.3365 / 0.3389

   Spot / 3 months 0.5622 / 0.5632

   Under the circumstances, is EUR ruling at a premium or at a discount against the USD?

   a. Premium

   b. Discount

5. The interbank USD JPY rates are as follows:

   Spot 144.22 / 144.72

   Spot / 1 month 12 / 10

   Spot / 2 months 24 / 21

   Spot / 3 months 39 / 36

   [Note: the swap points are given as pips. That is, 12 / 10 means JPY 0.12 / 0.10]

   Under the circumstances, is USD ruling at a premium or at a discount against the JPY?

   a. Premium

   b. Discount

Chapter 12

Convention of Quoting Forward Margins

12.1 QUOTING FORWARD MARGINS – MAJOR CURRENCIES

A pip, as has been explained earlier in chapter 8, is the 4th decimal place in a currency quote. Hence, if EUR USD = 1.1423, then '3' is the pip and if the EUR strengthens by 2 pips, then the new EUR USD quote would be 1.1425.

When dealing with forward margins, the terminology is slightly different.

Globally, forward margins are quoted in **Points,** and a point represents the smallest decimal movement in the currency quote.

For example,

EUR USD Spot: 1.1050, Forward margin: 25 points

Therefore, forward EUR USD rate = 1.1050 + 0.0025 = 1.1075

The forward margin here is being quoted as 25 points, which translates to 0.0025, which means that the forward margins are 1/10,000 of the value in points.

The reason for quoting the forward margins, as above, is because major currencies are quoted to 4 decimal places, for example, EUR USD = 1.1414, GBP USD = 1.3568, USD CHF = 0.7925, etc.

Check your Understanding

12.1 Spot EUR USD 1.1602

Spot / 1 month 17.0700

Spot / 2 months 33.2200

∴EUR USD 1-month forward = 1.1602 + (17.07÷10000) = 1.1602 + 0.0017 = 1.1619

And, EUR USD 2 months = 1.1602 + (33.22÷10000) = 1.1602 + 0.0033 = 1.1635

Check your Understanding

12.2 Spot USD HKD = 7.8237

Spot / 2 months (-) 239.20

Spot / 6 months (–) 631.10

(Margins are in negative as USD is at discount to HKD)

∴ USD HKD 2 months forward = 7.8237 – (239.2÷10000) = 7.8237 – 0.0239 = 7.7998

And, USD HKD 6 months forward = 7.8237 – (631.1÷10000) = 7.8237 – 0.0631 = 7.7606

12.2 QUOTING FORWARD MARGINS – JPY

The only major currency, which is an exception to the above convention is JPY. For example, USD JPY = 150.25, forward margin = (-) 35 points (negative, as USD is quoted as discount to JPY)

In this case, the forward USD JPY rate = 150.25 - 0.35 = 149.90

Hence, it can be seen that in the case of JPY, a point in the forward margin is 1/100th of a Yen, and not 1/10000th, as in the other major currencies earlier discussed.

The reason for the difference is that the quote for Yen, which is a low value currency, is up to 2 decimals only, for example 150.25 - and not up to 4 decimals.

Check your Understanding

12.3 Following are USD JPY exchange rates, and forward margins:

USD/JPY **159.04** +0.33 (+0.21%)

USDJPY 1M FWD	-42.6500
USDJPY 2M FWD	-82.3400
USDJPY 3M FWD	-125.6000
USDJPY 4M FWD	-163.1000
USDJPY 5M FWD	-202.9000
USDJPY 6M FWD	-244.1000

∴ USD JPY 1 month-forward = 159.04 – (42.6500÷100) = 159.04 – 0.43 = 158.61

And, USD JPY 3 months forward = 159.04 – (125.6÷100) = 159.04 – 1.26 = 157.78

12.3 QUOTING FORWARD MARGINS – INR

A third deviation to the convention of quoting forward points is the case in India, for example USD INR quotes.

As you have already learnt, USD INR pair is quoted up to 4 decimals, for example, USD INR = 91.5025 with the last 2 decimal places being in multiples of 25.

The above quote of USD INR = 91.5025, when expanded, means that 1 US Dollar = 91 Indian Rupee and 50.25 paise.

Forward margins for the USD INR are quoted in paise. Either rounded paise, eg., 12 paise or up to two decimals of paise, eg., 12.50 paise.

Therefore, in USD INR quote, forward margin of 12.50 means forward margin of 12.50 paise.

Hence if spot USD INR rate is 91.5025 and forward margin is 12.50, then USD INR forward rate = 91.5025 + 0.1250 = 91.6275.

Check your Understanding

12.4 Spot USD INR = 92.3050

Spot / 1 month – 15.75

∴ USD INR 1-month forward = 92.3050 + 0.1575 = 92.4625

Check your Understanding

12.5 Spot USD INR = 91.7775

Spot / 2 months = 23

∴ USD INR 2 months forward = 91.7775 + 0.2300 = 92.0075

Check your Understanding

12.6 Spot USD INR = 91.2650

Spot / 6 months = 113.25

∴ USD INR 2 months forward = 91.2650 + 1.1325 = 92.3975

Based on the conventions described in this chapter, a table containing representative currency pairs, their spot rates, forward margins and forward rates are provided below.

Currency Pair	Spot Quote Format	Decimal Places	1 Pip / Point	Forward Margin Quote	Forward Margin	Forward Rate
EUR/USD	1.1050	4	0.0001	Points/ Pips	+25	1.1075
GBP/USD	1.2705	4	0.0001	Points/ Pips	+30	1.2735
USD/CHF	0.8825	4	0.0001	Points/ Pips	-15	0.8810
AUD/USD	0.6550	4	0.0001	Points/ Pips	+20	0.6570
NZD/USD	0.6050	4	0.0001	Points/ Pips	+18	0.6068
USD/HKD	7.8125	4	0.0001	Points	-12	7.8113
USD/SGD	1.3450	4	0.0001	Points	-22	1.3428
USD/JPY	150.25	2	0.01	Points	-35	149.90
USD/INR	92.2550	2	0.0001	Paise	+12	92.3750

EXERCISE 12

1. Given the following GBP USD exchange rates and forward margins, calculate the two-month forward rate.

GBP/USD 1.3396 -0.0012

GBPUSD 1M FWD	-0.5200
GBPUSD 2M FWD	-2.2000
GBPUSD 3M FWD	-4.8400
GBPUSD 4M FWD	-8.6600
GBPUSD 5M FWD	-13.8300
GBPUSD 6M FWD	-20.6800

2. Given the following AUD USD exchange rates and forward margins, calculate the three-months forward rate.

AUD/USD 0.6970 -0.0027

AUDUSD 1M FWD	-2.9000
AUDUSD 2M FWD	-5.9200
AUDUSD 3M FWD	-9.7000
AUDUSD 4M FWD	-13.1000
AUDUSD 5M FWD	-17.5600
AUDUSD 6M FWD	-22.6200

3. Given the following USD CAD exchange rates and forward margins, calculate the six-months forward rate.

USD/CAD 1.3792 +0.0028 (

USDCAD 1M FWD	-19.1600
USDCAD 2M FWD	-36.3000
USDCAD 3M FWD	-54.4300
USDCAD 4M FWD	-72.2100
USDCAD 5M FWD	-88.6500
USDCAD 6M FWD	-104.7200

4. Given the following USD INR exchange rates and forward margins, calculate the 12-months forward rate.

Spot USD INR = 93.1025

USDINR 6M FWD	144.0000
USDINR 7M FWD	164.0000
USDINR 8M FWD	183.0000
USDINR 9M FWD	202.0000
USDINR 10M FWD	221.5000
USDINR 11M FWD	239.5000
USDINR 1Y FWD	261.5000

5. Given the following USD JPY exchange rates and forward margins, calculate the 3-months forward rate.

USD/JPY **158.91** +0.20 (+0.13%)

USDJPY 1M FWD	-42.8800
USDJPY 2M FWD	-82.5800
USDJPY 3M FWD	-126.0600
USDJPY 4M FWD	-163.1600
USDJPY 5M FWD	-202.9900
USDJPY 6M FWD	-244.9300

Chapter 13

Types of Foreign Exchange Rates

13.1 DIFFERENT TYPES OF RATES

There are four types of buying and selling exchange rates that we shall examine.

These are:

- TT Buying Rate
- TT Selling Rate
- Bill Buying Rate, and
- Bill Selling Rate.

As can be seen from the above list, while two are buying rates, the other two are selling rates. These are all Merchant Rates (as against Interbank Rates), since they are the rates at which banks buy or sell foreign currency from / to merchants (their customers).

The convention of merchant BUYING or SELLING rates is based upon what the situation is for the Banker in question. Hence, if the bank intends to BUY foreign currency from its customer, the rate that it will quote will be its BUYING rate, whereas if the bank intends to SELL foreign currency to its customer, the rate that it will be its SELLING rate.

Normally, banks would BUY foreign currencies from their exporters and customers receiving inward remittances, whereas banks would SELL foreign currencies to their importers and customer who send outward remittances.

13.2 TT BUYING RATE

Let us presume interbank USD INR rate of 90.10 / 90.20.

As per the above quoted rates, a bank can SELL USD - against INR - in the interbank (IB) market at the IB *buying* rate, ie., 90.10.

A bank can also BUY USD - against INR - in the interbank (IB) market at the IB *selling* rate, ie., 90.20.

Now, presume that an exporter customer approaches the Bank for selling export proceeds amounting to USD 100,000-, which has already been credited to the Bank's nostro account.

What will the Bank do?

The Bank will BUY USD 100,000- from the exporter and sell the USD 100,000- in the IB market in order to square its exchange position so as to avoid any exchange risk for itself.

Now, given the USD INR interbank rate of 90.10 / 90.20, the bank knows that it can sell USD 100,000- in the IB market at the IB buying rate, ie., 90.10. Hence, for USD 100,000, the Bank will receive INR 90,10,000- from the IB market. If it passed on the entire amount of INR 90,10,000- to the exporter, then the Bank would earn no profit for undertaking the transaction (ie., buying USD from the exporter and selling the USD in the IB market).

In order to earn some profit from the transaction, the Bank would, therefore, keep an amount of commission (called exchange margin or profit margin) of, say, 0.10% and pass on the balance amount to the exporter.

[Note: The rationale of keeping exchange margin has been detailed in Chapter 7 of this book.]

Since the Bank would pay the exporter LESS what it receives in the IB market, the exchange margin has to be DEDUCTED from the IB rate.

Hence, USD INR rate buying given to exporter = 90.10 less 0.10% = 90.01.

This rate so derived, USD INR = 90.01, is called the TT Buying Rate. It is the rate at which the Bank would buy USD from the exporter against INR, in those cases *where the bank's nostro account has already been credited.*

Therefore, the amount of INR which will be passed on by the Bank to the exporter would be:

100,000 x 90.01 = INR 90,01,000.

And the exchange profit that the Bank would earn on this transaction would be INR (90,10,000 less 90,00,000) = INR 9,000.

Rule 13.1: TT Buying Rate = IB Buying Rate LESS exchange margin.

TT buying rates are applicable for those transactions where the bank has already received credit in its nostro account. Examples of these are exports bills sent for collection and realised, proceeds of cheques which have been realised and clean inward remittances directly where the cover has been credited to the beneficiary bank's nostro account.

Check Your Understanding

13.1 Cosmic Exports has exported goods worth USD 10,000- to Magna Imports in Dubai. The documents are presented to Cosmic Exports' bank on 10th December, 2025, with a request to pay them on realisation of the bill.

The documents are remitted by the exporter's bank to the bank in Dubai and paid by the importers on 20th December 2025. The nostro account of the exporter's bank is credited with USD 10,000- on 21st December, 2025.

The following are the Interbank USD INR rates on 21st Dec, 2025 and the bank recovers a margin of 0.05% as its exchange profit.

Spot USD INR 89.7800 / 7900

What is the rate that the bank will quote to Cosmic Exports?

Exchange rate quoted to Cosmic Exports (TT Buying rate) =

89.7800 less 0.05% = 89.7800 – 0.0449 = 89.7351, or **89.73**.

Check Your Understanding

13.2 Mr Jacob is a Doctor in USA and he has remitted USD 5,000- through his bankers, Bank of America, NY to his father, Mathew, who maintains his savings bank account with Bank of India, Jamshedpur.

Bank of America has credited the amount of USD 5,000- to the nostro account of Bank of India.

The interbank USD INR spot rate is 88.6525 / 50

If Bank of India keeps exchange margin of INR 0.50 on the transaction, what is the amount that the bank will credit to the SB account of Mr Mathew?

[Note: Exchange margin of INR 0.50 means INR 0.50 per USD Dollar]

The TT buying rate that Bank of India will apply =

88.6525 less 0.50 = 88.6525 – 0.4433 = 88.2092, or 88.20

The amount credited to Mathew's SB account = 5,000 x 88.20 = INR 4,41,000- .

13.3 TT SELLING RATE

This is quite similar, in principle, to TT Buying Rate. However, TT Selling Rate is the merchant rate that Banks quote to customers to whom the Bank proposes to *sell* foreign currency, eg., importers.

Let us presume the same interbank USD INR rate of 90.10 / 90.20. As per the said rates, a bank can BUY USD, against INR, in the interbank (IB) market at the IB selling rate, ie., 90.20.

Now, presume that an importer customer approaches the Bank for buying USD 100,000-, which it requires in order to make payment of an import bill.

What will the Bank do?

The Bank will SELL USD 100,000- to the importer, after buying the USD 100,000- in the IB market.

Now, for buying USD 100,000- in the IB market at the IB selling rate, ie., 90.20, the bank will require an amount of INR 90,20,000. For doing that, if the Bank recovered exactly INR 90,20,000 from the importer, the Bank would earn no profit for undertaking the transaction (ie., buying USD from the IB market and selling the USD to the importer customer).

In order to earn some profit from the transaction, the Bank would, therefore, keep an amount of commission (exchange margin) of, say, 0.15%. It would, therefore, recover an INR amount equivalent to USD 100,000- PLUS the exchange margin of 0.15% from the importer customer.

Hence, USD INR rate given by the Bank to the importer

= 90.20 plus 0.15% = 90.20 + 0.1353 = 90.3353, or, **90.34.**

This rate so derived, USD INR = 90.34, is called the TT Selling Rate. It is the rate at which the Bank would sell USD to the importer against INR.

Therefore, the amount of INR which will be recovered by the Bank from the importer would be:

100,000 x 90.34 = INR 90,34,000

And the exchange profit that the Bank would earn on this transaction would be INR (90,34,000 less 90,20,000) = INR 14,000.

Rule 13.2: TT Selling Rate = IB Selling Rate PLUS exchange margin.

Examples of transactions where TT selling rates are applicable are clean outward remittances.

Check Your Understanding

13.3 Ms Nutan requires to remit USD 12,000- as fees to a University in Singapore, for pursuing her Master's degree there.

If the interbank USD INR spot rate prevailing is 89.5650 / 75 and the bank keeps exchange profit margin of 0.15%, what is the amount of INR that will be debited by the bank to Ms Nutan's account in order to make the remittance?

Spot USD INR = 89.5650 / 75

TT selling rate = 89.5675 plus 0.15%

= 89.5675 + 0.1344 = 89.7019, or 89.71

Amount in INR that the bank will recover = 12,000 x 89.71 = INR 10,76,520-.

13.4 BILL BUYING RATE

You will have observed that when it was examined how to derive TT Buying Rate, one of the assumptions was that the export proceeds were already credited to the Bank's nostro account, ie., the foreign currency funds were already available to the Bank.

While learning about Bill Buying Rate, it is necessary to first, be familiar with two concepts related to international trade, viz., Normal Transit Period (NTP) and tenor of an export bill.

- ***Normal Transit Period (NTP)***

  NTP is the number of days that it is expected to take between the day an export bill, drawn on sight basis, is purchased by the Bank and the day the proceeds are expected to be credited to the exporter's bank's nostro account (ie., after the bill is paid by the importer and proceeds of the bill are remitted by the importer's bank to the exporter's bank's nostro account).

  [Note: Purchase of a bill by a bank means the act of the bank making an advance to the customer, against the bill in question.]

  The NTP depends on various factors, viz., the currency of the bill, type of reimbursement provided, etc.

  However, for sake of simplicity let us take the NTP to be 25 days, as 25 days is the NTP specified by Foreign Exchange Dealers Association of India (FEDAI) for realisation of foreign currency bills. It is seen that the NTP of most export transactions come under this category of 25 days.

- ***Tenor of Export Bill***

  Export bills are the documents that an exporter submits to his / her banker so that the same may be sent to importer in order to demand payment for the goods supplied. These consist of documents like bill of exchange, commercial invoice, bill of lading, airway bill, packing list, weight list, insurance policy, etc.

  The terms of payment may be for the importer to pay immediately upon receipt of documents (called Payment at Sight, or also Documents against Payment – DP).

  Alternatively, the terms of payment may provide the importer some time to make payment, after receipt of the documents. The time so provided for payment is called the usance period and can be any number of days as mutually agreed and contracted between the exporter and importer – 15 days, 30 days, 45, days, 60 days, 90 days, etc. Such bills are called usance bills, with the payment being due at the end of the usance period (called maturity date or due date).

  Such bills are also called DA bills (Documents against Acceptance), because the importer obtains delivery of the documents after furnishing his or her acceptance to make payment of the bill on its maturity date.

  A usance bill can, initially, have an unknown maturity date, which becomes known only after the importer "sights" the bill (for example, a bill drawn at 30 days after sight, or 30 days after acceptance) or it can, ab initio, have a fixed maturity date (for example, if it is drawn at 30 days from date of bill of lading or linked to any other date which is known when the documents are submitted by the exporter to the bank).

13.4.1 Bill Buying Rate for Sight Bills

Coming back to concept of bill buying rate, take the case of a sight (DP) export bill which is tendered by an exporter to the Bank and for which the exporter requires immediate payment of INR equivalent, ie., before the bill is sent to the importer's bank in the foreign country and, therefore, before the exporter's Bank receives the export proceeds in its nostro account.

This type of transaction, as you have observed earlier, is known as "purchase of an export bill".

In such a case, the exporter's bank will send the documents to the importer's bank for payment by the importer and it will expect to receive the export proceeds in its nostro account only at the end of the NTP, ie., after 25 days.

If the exporter's bank has to honour the request of the exporter to purchase the bill and pay the INR immediately (and not wait for 25 days - by which time its nostro account is expected to be credited), it will have to quote to the exporter, not the TT buying rate (which is based on the spot rate), but a 25 day *forward buying rate*.

However, forward rates are not quoted for odd periods like 25 days, and hence the exporter's bank will require to base its bill buying rate on the forward rate for the particular month when the amount is expected to be credited to its nostro account.

Let us understand this, by way, of an example.

ABC Exports submits an export bill for purchase (ie., immediate payment in INR) for USD 50,000- on 10th January 2026, to its bankers, Commercial Bank. The USD INR spot rates prevailing on 10/1/2026 are as follows:

Spot 90.10 / 20

Spot / January 30/35

Spot / February 40/45

Spot / March 55/60

Spot / April 62/67

Spot / May 70/75

Since the exporter has tendered the bill for purchase on 10/1/2026, its proceeds are expected to be received only on 4th February (ie., after 25 days following 10/1/2026).

Hence, the applicable rate would be the USD INR February forward rate, ie., (90.10 + 0.40) = 90.50. This is because, from the forward margins listed in this example, it is clear that USD is at a premium compared to INR and, hence, the premium of 40 paise (INR 0.40) has to be added to the spot buying rate 90.10.

However, the premium of 40 paise is the premium *till the end of February (ie., 28/2/2026*) whereas the export proceeds are expected to be received much earlier, on 4/2/2026). Hence, the Bank would not pass on the premium for the full month of February to the exporter, but would rather pass on only the premium till end of January (ie., 31/1/2026) to the exporter.

Therefore, the USD INR rate bill buying rate that the Bank would quote to ABC Exports would be:

90.10 + 0.30 (premium up to January) = 90.40

If the bank keeps exchange margin of 0.10%, the effective rate would be 90.40 – 0.10%,

ie., 90.40 – 0.0904 = 90.3096, or 90.30

Suppose, in the above example, the USD was at a discount to INR and the rates were are follows:

Spot 90.10 / 20

Spot / January 30/25

Spot / February 40/35

Spot / March 55/50

Spot / April 62/57

Spot / May 70/65

In such a case, using the same principle that the Bank would extract maximum from the exporter, the bill buying rate would include the discount - not till end of January - but till end of February and its bill buying rate for the transaction would be:

90.10 – 40* = 89.70

* Discount till end of February.

Furthermore, if the bank keeps exchange margin of 0.10%, the effective rate would be 89.70 – 0.10%,

ie., 89.70 – 0.0897 = 89.6103, or **89.61**

In both the above cases, since the bank is expected to credit the account of the exporter with INR on 10/1/2026, whereas it will receive the proceeds only on 4/2/2026, it will separately recover interest for the 25 days period at its export credit interest rate.

Rule13.3: Bill Buying Rate for Sight Bills:

= IB Buying Rate

(+) Premium or (-) Discount (for NTP)

(-) exchange margin

Check Your Understanding

13.4 Novelty Exports has submitted an export bill amounting to USD 25,000- to its bankers, on 10th November, 2025 with a request to purchase the same and credit their current account, immediately.

The USD INR rates prevailing on 10th Nov, 2025 are as follows:

Spot USD INR 88.7675/7700

Spot / November 15 / 12

Spot / December 33 / 31

Spot / January 44 / 41

Spot February 52 / 50

What is the Bill Buying rate that will be quoted by the bank, presuming that the bank will recover exchange profit margin of 0.10%?

Taking NTP to be 25 days, the due date of the bill would be 5th December 2025.

Since, the forward margins are in descending order, the USD is being quoted at a discount to INR.

As such, the bank would levy discount for full month of December and the bill buying rate would be,

88.7675 – 0.3300 = 88.4375

Recovering exchange margin of 0.10%, the bill buying rate would be:

88.4375 - 0.10% = 88.4375 - 0.0884 = 88.349, or **88.34.**

13.4.2 *Bill Buying Rate for Usance Bills*

For usance bills, the calculation methodology is quite similar to sight bills – the only difference being that the interim period between crediting the exporter's account and receiving credit of bill proceeds is the NTP plus the usance period.

Hence, in the previous example of ABC Exports contained in section 13.4.1, if the bill for USD 50,000- purchased on 10/1/2026 was payable 60 days after sight, then the due date would be (25+60), ie., 85 days from 10/1/2026, ie., 5th April 2026.

Assuming USD to be at a premium against the INR, the bank would load premium up to the earlier month (ie., March) on to the spot buying rate and the bill buying rate for such a bill would be:

90.10 + 0.55 = 90.65

If the bank keeps exchange margin of 0.10%, the effective rate would be 90.65 – 0.10%,

ie., 90.65 – 0.0907 = 90.5593, or **90.55.**

And, if we assume that the USD was at a discount against the INR, the bank would deduct discount up to end of April from the spot buying rate and the bill buying rate for such a bill would be:

- 0.62 = 89.48

Furthermore, if the bank keeps exchange margin of 0.10%, the effective rate would be 89.48 – 0.10%,

ie., 89.40 – 0.0895 = 89.3105, or **89.31.**

Rule 13.4: Bill Buying Rate for Usance Bills:

= IB Buying Rate

(+) Premium or (-) Discount (for NTP *and Usance Period, if any*)

(-) exchange margin

Check Your Understanding

13.5 Arati Exports has tendered a bill for USD 35,000- to their bankers on 29th September, 2025. The bill of exchange is drawn at 60 days after sight and the exporters want their bank to discount the same and credit the proceeds to their account.

[Note: Whilst making immediate payment of an export bill constitutes purchase, when the same is done for a usance bill, the terminology is "discounting".]

The USD INR exchange rates prevailing on the said day, are as follows:

Spot 86.4500 / 25

Spot / September 05/08

Spot / October 15 / 17

Spot / November 27 / 30

Spot / December 38 / 41

Spot / January 49 / 53

What is the bill buying rate that will be quoted by the bank, presuming that the bank will recover exchange profit margin of 0.15%?

Taking NTP to be 25 days and usance period of 60 days (total 85 days), the due date of the bill would be 23rd December 2025.

Since, the forward margins are in ascending order, the USD is being quoted at a premium to INR.

As such, the bank would pass on premium only till November end and the bill buying rate would be,

86.4500 + 0.2700 = 86.7200

Keeping an exchange profit margin of 0.15%, the bill buying rate that the bank will quote to Arati Exports will be,

less 0.15% = 86.72 - 0.1301 = 86.5899. or **86.58.**

13.5 BILL SELLING RATE

The concept of bill selling rate is very simple and it is used when import bills are paid and their proceeds are remitted. Bill Selling rate is derived from the prevailing TT selling rate by adding the commission of the bank for handling the import documents.

Therefore, if the prevailing TT selling rate is 90.2500 and the bank's handling commission is 0.50%, then the bill selling rate =

90.2500 + 0.50% = 90.2500 + 0.4513 = 90.7013, or 90.71

Rule 13.5: Bill Selling Rate = TT Selling Rate PLUS bill handling commission.

Check Your Understanding

13.6 Premium Imports has instructed its bankers to make payment of an import bill for USD 100,000-.

The prevailing interbank USD INR rates are as follows, and the bank charges 0.15% as exchange margin and commission of 0.35% for handling the document handling:

Spot USD INR 90.6600 / 6650

Calculate the TT Selling and Bill Selling rates.

TT selling rate = 90.6650 + 0.15% = 90.6650 + 0.1360 = 90.8010, or **90.81.**

Bill selling rate = 90.81 + 0.35% = 90.81 + 0.3178 = 91.1278, or **91.13.**

EXERCISE 13

1. A 60 days usance export bill for USD 20,000- sent by bankers of Advent Exports was credited to the bank's nostro account on 12th Jan 2026.

   The USD INR inter-bank rates on that day were are follows:

   Spot 91.2025 / 50

   Assuming that the bank retains 0.15% as exchange profit margin, what is the rate that the bank will provide to the exporter?

2. Mr Ganesh received a wire transfer on 18th March 2026, amounting to EUR 1,500- from his son in France.

   The interbank rates prevailing on that day were as under:

   Spot USD INR 92.3050/75

   Spot EUR USD 1.1467 / 69

   Assuming that the bank retains 0.25% as exchange margin, what is the rate that Mr Ganesh can obtain from the Bank?

3. Akash Exports submitted an export bill, drawn payable at sight and amounting to USD 125,000- to its bankers on 12th March 2026 with a request to purchase the same and credit their current account.

   The USD INR rates and forward margins prevailing in the interbank market on that day were as follows:

Spot USD INR 92.2000/25

Spot / March 06 / 08

Spot / April 15 / 18

Spot / May 29 / 31

Spot / June 38 / 40

Assuming that the bank retains 0.10% as exchange profit margin, what is the rate that the bank will provide to the exporter?

4. Dolly Enterprises submitted an export bill amounting to USD 20,000- to its bankers for discounting on 12th March 2026. The bill was drawn payable at 90 days from date of bill of lading and the bill of lading was dated 4th March 2026.

   The USD INR rates prevailing in the interbank market on 12th March were as follows:

   Spot USD INR 91.6775 / 6800

   Spot / March 10 / 12

   Spot / April 20 / 22

   Spot / May 36 / 37

   Spot / June 45 / 47

   Spot / July 55 / 57

   Assuming that the bank retains 0.15% as exchange profit margin, what is the rate that the bank will provide to the exporter?

5. Omega Industries submitted an export bill amounting to USD 265,000-, drawn at 60 days sight to its bankers, on 11th September 2025 for discounting.

   The USD INR rates prevailing in the interbank market on 12th March were as follows:

   Spot USD INR 88.7325 / 50

   Spot / 1 month 12 / 10

   Spot / 2 months 20 / 18

   Spot / 3 months 29 / 26

   Spot / 4 months 39 / 37

   Assuming that the bank retains 0.05% as exchange profit margin, what is the rate that the bank will provide to the exporter?

6. In the above transaction, if the export credit interest rate of interest is 9.35% pa, and the bank deducts a margin of 25% as per terms of sanction, what is the amount that will be credited to the exporter's current account?

7. Magma Industries, which is in the business of manufacturing printing machinery, has decided to place an advertisement in one of the industry magazines, which is published from Dubai. For the said advertisement, the company has to remit an amount of USD 2,500-.

   The interbank rates prevailing on that day were:

   Spot USD INR 91.5675 / 5700

Assuming that the bank retains 0.25% as exchange profit margin, what is the exchange rate that the bank will provide to Magma Industries?

8. Cosmos Industries has requested its bankers to remit the proceeds of an import bill for CHF 32,500-.

   Assuming that:

   Spot USD INR is 91.2225 / 50

   Spot USD CHF is 0.7912 / 16

   Exchange profit margin retained by the bank is 0.20%, and

   Bill handling commission is charged at 0.40%

   What is the amount that would be debited by the bank to the current account of the importer?

Chapter 14

Cross Currency Forward Rates

So far, you have learnt how to calculate various types of merchant rates (TT Buying, TT Selling, Bill Buying and Bill Selling) where the currency pairs used has been USD and INR. There is a reason for that – for, after all, the USD INR is the most commonly used and quoted currency pair in India, accounting for about 96% of the quotes!

However, there are other quoted currency pairs also, viz., EUR INR, GBP INR, JPY INR, SGD INR, CAD INR, etc.

Although these pairs are represented in fewer forex quotes, they are, nevertheless, important and one should know how to calculate the various types of rates for such pairs also.

While in an earlier chapter, you have already learnt how to calculate cross rates, using the Chain Rule, the emphasis will be paid on cross currency forward rates.

14.1 CROSS CURRENCY FORWARD RATES (BUYING)

The methodology of calculating currency buying rates is simple – first calculate the basic FCY INR rate for the said currency, using the Chain Rule, and then load the exchange margin and forward premium / discount (if the rate entails forwards, like export bills).

Example:

Calculate the TT buying rate for EUR, given the following ruling spot rates, and given that the bank levies exchange margin of 0.10%:

USD INR = 90.5725 / 50

EUR USD = 1.1822 / 24

EUR INR TT Buying cross rate using Chain Rule = (90.5725 x 1.1822) – 0.10%

= 107.0748 – 0.10% = 107.0748 – 0.1071 = 106.9677, or **106.96**

Example:

Calculate the JPY INR bill buying rate for discounting an export bill, with tenor of 60 days after sight.

The exchange rate / forward margins are as follows and the bank levies exchange margin of 0.15% on the rate.

Spot USD INR = 90.5725 / 50

Spot USD JPY = 153.36 / 154.10

Forward margins

USD INR

Spot / 1 month 26 / 28

Spot / 2 months 38 / 40

Spot / 3 months 49 / 51

Spot / 4 months 60 / 62

USD JPY

Spot / 1 month 36.51 / 35.91

Spot / 2 months 77.94 / 77.66

Spot / 3 months 114.25 / 113.25

Spot / 4 month 156.41 / 152.25

[It should be noted here that the forward margins for USD JPY here are quoted in fraction of Japanese Yens, ie., 35.51 means 0.3551 yen and 114.25 means 1.1425 Yen.]

Moreover, the USD JPY forward margins are quoted in descending order, which means that the JPY is being quoted a **discount** to USD.

Step 1 – calculate for forward period to be reckoned for the calculations

Step 2 – calculate the USD INR forward rate for the said period

Step 3 - calculate the USD JPY forward rate for the said period

Step 4 – calculate the JPY INR forward cross rate, using the obtained two forward rates

Step 5 – load the exchange margin and derive the merchant Bill Buying rate.

Accordingly, the example given in this section is worked out, as follows.

Step 1 – Calculate the forward period

Forward period of the export bill = 60 days usance + 25 days NTP, ie., 85 days (ie., more than 2 months, less than 3 months).

Since this is an export (purchase) transaction, the premium will be reckoned for 2 months and discount will be reckoned for 3 months, in the calculations.

[Reason: The bank will pass on the lowest possible rate to the exporter customer].

Step 2 – Calculate the forward USD INR rate

USD INR forward rate

Spot USD INR = 90.5725 / 90.5750

Spot / 2 months = 0.38 / 0.40 (add)

Forward USD INR rate = 90.9525 / 90.9750

Step 3 - calculate the forward USD JPY rate

USD JPY forward rate

Spot USD JPY = 153.36 / 154.10

Spot / 3 months = 1.1425 / 1.1325 (subtract)

Forward USD JPY rate = 152.2175 / 152.9675, or 152.21 / 152.97

Step 4 - calculate the forward JPY INR rate

Forward USD INR = 90.9525 / 90.9750

Forward USD JPY = 152.21 / 152.97

Forward cross rate, JPY INR = 90.9525 ÷ 152.97 = 0.5946 or 100 JPY = INR 59.46

Step 5 – calculate the JPY INR Bill Buying rate

Bill buying rate = 59.46 – 0.15% = 59.46 – 0.0892 = 59.3708, or **59.37**

Check Your Understanding

14.1

On 15th January 2026, Cosmic Exports submitted a sight bill for SGD 12,500 to its bankers for purchase.

Given the following rates and given that the bank retains exchange margin of 0.15%, calculate the SGD Bill Buying Rate.

USD INR

Spot 90.2475 / 2500

Spot / Jan 12 / 15

Spot / Feb 28 / 30

Spot / Mar 38 / 41

USD SGD

Spot 1.2624 / 2704

Spot / Jan 25 / 24

Spot / Feb 53 / 52

Spot / Mar 79 / 78

Due date for sight bill (NTP 25 days) = 9/2/2026. Being an export bill, bank will reckon premium only till end of Jan 2026 for USD but will reckon discount till end of Feb 2026 for SGD.

Therefore, forward USD INR rate = (90.2475 + 0.12 / 90.2500 + 0.15) = 90.3675 / 90.4000

And, forward USD SGD rate = (1.2624 – 0.0053 / 1.2704 – 0.0052) = 1.2571 / 1.2652

Therefore, forward cross buying rate for SGD INR = 90.3675 ÷1.2652 = 71.4255

And, **bill buying rate for SGD INR** = 71.4255 – 0.15% = 71.4255 – 0.1071 = 71.3184,

or **71.31.**

14.2 CROSS CURRENCY FORWARD RATES (SELLING)

For calculating the cross currency selling rates also, the methodology of calculating is simple – first calculate the basic FCY INR selling rate for the said currency, using the Chain Rule, and then load the exchange margin and bill handling commission (if the rate entails handling of import bills).

Example:

Calculate the TT Selling rate for an outward remittance of GBP 75,000, given the following exchange rates and given that the bank retains exchange margin of 0.20%.

USD INR 90.6700 / 25

GBP USD 1.3550 / 3650

GBP INR cross rate using Chain Method = (90.6725 x 1.3650) + 0.20%

= 123.7680 + 0.20% = 123.7680 + 0.2475 = 124.0155, or **124.02**

Check Your Understanding

14.2

Calculate the forward AUD INR rate for sending an outward remittance after 3 months, given the following exchange rates and given that the bank retains exchange margin of 0.20%.

Spot USD INR = 90.5725 / 50

Spot AUD USD = 0.7086 / 0.7126

Forward margins

USD INR

Spot / 1 month 26 / 28

Spot / 2 months 38 / 40

Spot / 3 months 49 / 51

Spot / 4 months 60 / 62

AUD USD

Spot / 1 month 0.9900 / 0.6300

Spot / 2 months 2.2200 / 1.9200

Spot / 3 months 4.6600 / 4.3100

Spot / 4 months 7.3900 / 8.8400

USD INR 3 months forward selling rate = (90.5750 + 0.51) = 91.0850

AUD USD 3 months forward selling rate = (0.7126 – 0.000431) = 0.712169, or 0.7122

Accordingly, AUD INR 3 month forward selling rate = 91.0850 x 0.7122 = 64.8707

And AUD INR 3-month forward merchant selling rate = 64.8707 + 0.20% = 64.8707 + 0.1297

= 65.0004, or **65.01.**

Check Your Understanding

14.3

Calculate the CAD INR rate for retirement and remittance of proceeds of a usance import bill for CAD 55,000, which is due 3 months from today, given the exchange rates as follows and given that bank retains 0.20% as exchange margin and 0.40% as bill handling commission.

Spot USD INR = 90.5725 / 50

Spot USD CAD = 1.3682 / 1.3705

Forward margins

USD INR

Spot / 1 month 26 / 28

Spot / 2 months 38 / 40

Spot / 3 months 49 / 51

USD CAD

Spot / 1 month 16.3600 / 16.1100

Spot / 2 months 34.4500 / 34.1000

Spot / 3 months 53.5000 / 53.1700

USD INR 3 months forward selling rate = (90.5750 + 0.51) = 91.0850

[Note: premium for 3 months added to spot USD INR selling rate]

USD CAD 3 months forward buying rate = (1.3682 - 0.005350) = 1.36285, or 1.3629

[Note: discount for 3 months subtracted from spot USD CAD buying rate]

∴ CAD INR 3 months selling rate = (91.0850 ÷ 1.3629) = 66.8318

And, CAD INR 3 months merchant forward selling rate = 66.8318 + 0.20% = 66.8318 + 0.1337 = 66.9655

And, CAD INR 3 months bill selling rate = 66.9655 + 0.40% = 66.9655 + 0.2679 = 67.2334,

or **67.24**

[Note: the rounding off to two decimals, while quoting bills selling rate takes place only at the final stage and not at the intermediate stage when merchant Forward Selling rate is derived (in this example, 66.7719) since the rate is not quoted to the customer at the Merchant Forward Selling rate stage, but instead only at the Forward Bill Selling stage.]

EXERCISE 14

1. Ajanta Exports had exported garments to Belgium and submitted documents on 15th January 2026, for EUR 5,600-, which are drawn at 60 days after sight. They were not interested in discounting the bill and had requested the bank to send the same to the buyers on collection basis.

   In order to protect the company against exchange fluctuations, the exporter requested the bank to quote forward rate for receipt of the Euro proceeds.

   Given the following prevailing interbank rates and forward margins, calculate the appropriate EUR INR rate that the bank can quote to the exporter.

   Assume that the bank retains profit margin of 0.10% on the quote.

   Spot USD INR 90.3650/75

   Spot / I month 12 / 14

   Spot / 2 months 21 / 23

   Spot / 3 months 30 / 32

   Spot / 4 months 44 / 45

   Spot EUR USD 1.1624 / 26

   Spot / 1 month 17.32 / 17.52

   Spot / 2 months 32.96 / 35.56

   Spot / 3 months 49.24 / 50.94

   Spot / 4 months 62.85 / 63.44

2. Cambrian Exports had submitted an export bill for HKD 15,000- to its bankers on 15th January 2026, with a request to discount the same and credit the proceeds to their current account. The bill is drawn at 30 days after sight.

   Given the following rates and forward margins ruling in the interbank market, calculate the rate which the bank can quote to the exporter for discounting the bill.

   Assume that the bank retains profit margin of 0.15% on the quote.

   Spot USD INR 90.3650/75

   Spot / I month 12 / 14

   Spot / 2 months 21 / 23

   Spot / 3 months 30 / 32

   Spot USD HKD 7.7973 / 80

   Spot / I month 142.65 / 139.65

   Spot / 2 months 270.40 / 267.40

   Spot / 3 months 370.60 / 367.60

3. Benzer & Co has entered into a technology transfer with Paramount Ltd of Australia and is required to remit license fees amounting to AUD 12,500- in in May 2026.

   They contacted their bankers on 21st March 2026, and requested them to quote the appropriate AUD INR rate for conducting the transfer at the future date.

Given the following rates and forward margins ruling in the interbank market, calculate the rate which the bank can quote to Benzer & Co for making the remittance in May 2026.

Assume that the bank retains profit margin of 0.20% on the quote.

Spot USD INR 92.2025 / 50

Spot / March 12 / 14

Spot / April 22 / 23

Spot / May 33 / 35

Spot / June 42 / 44

Spot AUD USD 0.7011 / 15

Spot / March 1.19 / 1.04

Spot / April 6.02 / 5.82

Spot / May 9.47 / 9.27

Spot / June 13.66 / 13.16

4. Importex India has received an import bill for GBP 32,500 which is drawn on 90 days after sight.

   The bill has been accepted by Importex on 18th March 2026, to mature on 16th June 2026.

   Given the following rates and forward margins ruling in the interbank market, calculate the rate which the bank can quote to the importer for remitting proceeds of the bill on due date?

   Assume that the bank retains profit margin of 0.20% on the quote and also levies handling commission of 0.35%.

Spot USD INR 92.1225 / 50

Spot / March 06 / 06

Spot / April 21 / 23

Spot / May 29 / 31

Spot / June 39 / 41

Spot GBP USD 1.3533 / 35

Spot / March 0.65 / 0.27

Spot / April 2.71 / 1.11

Spot / May 5.55 / 2.94

Spot / June 10.23 / 6.84

Chapter 15

Forward Contracts: Concepts

15.1 WHAT IS A FORWARD CONTRACT

You have learnt what forward rates are. They are rates quoted for, a foreign currency, in transactions where the settlement period is beyond spot, ie., beyond 2 business days.

As an extension of that concept, a forward contract is a contract where a bank agrees, today, to quote an exchange rate for a foreign currency for a future date.

For example, if the prevailing USD INR spot buying rate on 10/1/2026 is 90.1050 and the bank agrees to quote a rate for USD INR at 90.6075 for delivery 2 months from today, ie., on 10/3/2026, and signs an agreement to that effect with the customer, then it has entered into a Forward Contract.

The following figure illustrates the concept of a forward contract.

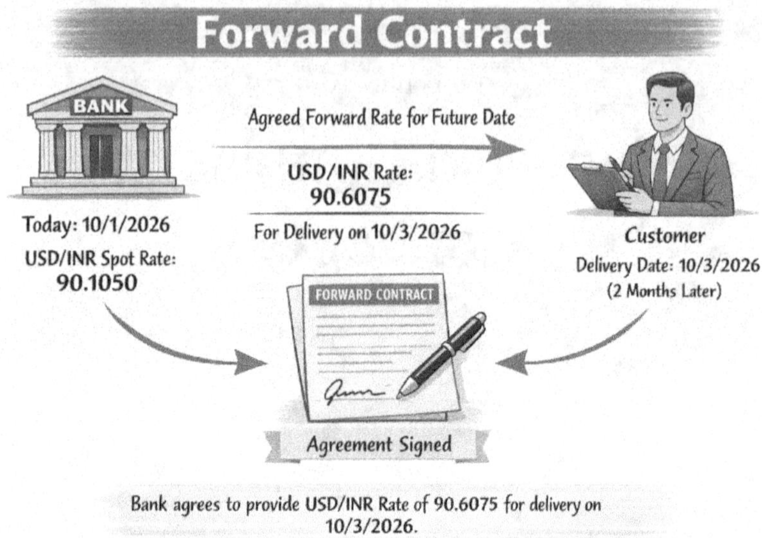

Figure 15.1 Concept of forward contract

A similar rate can also be quoted for selling any foreign currency, at a future date.

15.2 FORWARD CONTRACTS WITH FIXED AND OPTIONAL MATURITY

In terms of FEDAI Rules, all forward contracts are booked, either, for a fixed future maturity date, or with an option period of delivery, provided that the option period does not exceed one month.

- Example – fixed date forward contract – USD INR contract with maturity date 15th February 2026.
- Example – option delivery forward contract – USD INR contract available for utilisation from 10th February 2026 to 9th March 2026 (an entire month).

In all cases of forward contracts with delivery options, the right to exercise the option lies with the customer.

Given the definition of a forward contract, it is, therefore, a financial instrument using which a customer can be free from the fluctuations in foreign exchange rates.

In the foregoing example, on 10/3/2026, irrespective of whether the spot USD INR is lower than 90.6075 or higher than 90.6075, the customer will be able to utilise the USD INR rate of 90.6075, which was provided by the bank two months ago.

A forward contract, therefore, gives the customer the right to buy or sell a foreign currency at the pre-determined exchange rate. However, it also places upon the customer the obligation to buy or sell a foreign currency at the contracted exchange rate.

Hence, irrespective of what the prevailing exchange rate is on 10/3/2026, the customer must buy USD from (or sell USD to) the bank at the contracted rate, which in this example is 90.6075.

Since a forward contract gives the customer the right, as well as imposes an obligation on the customer to transact at the contracted rate, there may be a few different types of scenarios that are possible.

These are:

- Delivery on due date
- Early delivery of the forward contract
- Cancellation of the forward contract
- Extension of the forward contract

This chapter has covered the concept of forward contracts and will also, in the following section, explain what constitutes Delivery on due date.

The other three scenarios, which entail various types of charges and costs, have been separated and covered in subsequent chapters, in order that they can be explained in detail.

15.3 FORWARD CONTRACTS – DELIVERY ON DUE DATE

A delivery of a forward contract on due date, is one which takes place:

- During the option period, in the case of a forward contract which can be utilised over a period of time,

  [say, a forward contract with delivery option between 1st March and 31st March, delivered on 12th March]

  or

- One which takes place on the maturity / expiry date, in the case of a fixed-date forward contract.

  [say, a forward contract with maturity date 15th March, delivered on 15th March.]

Chapter 16

Early Delivery

16.1 WHAT IS EARLY DELIVERY

Early delivery of a forward contract is one in which:

- For a fixed date delivery contract – delivery of the foreign currency takes place before the fixed maturity / expiry date, or
- For an option delivery contract – delivery of the foreign currency takes place prior to the commencement of the option period

For example, a forward contract that is utilised (ie., delivered) on 20th March, for a fixed-date forward contract which expires on 5th April. Or, a forward contract that is utilised on 20th March for a contract which can be used any time during the month of April.

It is in the bank's discretion whether to accept or not to accept, a request from its customer for early delivery of foreign exchange under a forward contract.

The bank can accept the request, provided the customer agrees to pay the costs, if any, that are related to early delivery of the contract.

Now:

- what are these costs,
- why do they occur, and
- how are they computed.

To answer these questions, one must understand what happens when a customer books a forward contract and thereafter, requests for early delivery of the contract.

16.2. MECHANISM OF EARLY DELIVERY

The mechanism of early delivery under a forward contract is illustrated by the following example.

Example:

On 1st June, 2025, Orbit Exports receives a mail from its buyers in Dubai, that they will remit proceeds of an export bill amounting to USD 75,000- during October, 2025.

Therefore, on 1st June 2025, Orbit Exports requests its bank to book a forward purchase contract for USD 75,000- with maturity October 2025 (ie., optional delivery on any business day between 1st Oct and 31st Oct, 2025).

The proceeds of the export bill are, however, received early – say, on 19th August, 2025. Accordingly, the exporters request the bank to accept early delivery of the forward contract, and the bank agrees to do so.

The USD INR rates of various dates are, as follows:

1st June 2025

Spot USD INR 82.6250 / 75
Spot / June 12 / 15
Spot / July 22 / 24
Spot / August 34 / 38
Spot / September 48 / 51
Spot / October 55 / 58

19th August

Spot USD INR 83.2225 / 50
Spot / August 06 / 09
Spot / September 21 / 24
Spot / October 30 / 32
Spot / November 43 / 46

Interest on inflow of funds: 4% pa
Interest on outlay of funds: 8% pa
Exchange margin of the Bank: 0.15%

MECHANICS OF THE TRANSACTIONS

a. On 1/6/2025

The customer books forward purchase contract for USD 75,000- delivery October 2025. From the forward margins available, it can be seen that the USD is at premium to INR and, therefore, the bank will pass on premium only till September 2025.

Hence, the merchant forward USD INR rate, delivery October, 2025 (1st Oct to 31st Oct) =

82.6250 + 0.48 = 83.1050 less margin, 0.15%

= 83.1050 – 0.1247 = 82.9803, or 82.98

Since the bank is booking a forward contract for the exporter, it expects that it will receive USD 75,000 from the exporter during October 2025. Moreover, having quoted the forward buying rate to the customer, the bank has assumed an overbought position of USD 75,000 for October 2025.

Therefore, in order to eliminate exchange risk, and assuming that the customer will deliver the USD amount on 31st October 2025, the bank will book a forward sale contract in the interbank market at the IB October buying rate, ie., 83.1750 (82.6250 + 0.5500).

The logic here is that when the exporter surrenders USD 75,000 to the bank during October, 2025, the bank will purchase it from the exporter at the merchant contracted rate of 82.98 and immediately sell it in the interbank market at the IB contracted rate of 83.1750 (and, thereby make a profit of INR 0.1950, or 19.50 paise per USD).

This part of the transaction is depicted by the following figures 15.1 and 15.2.

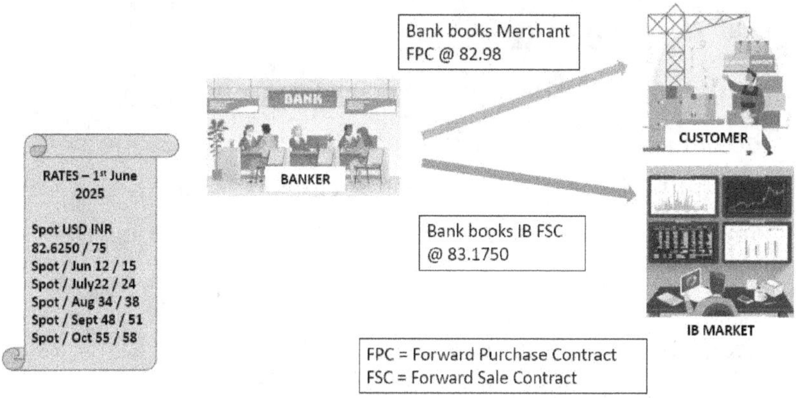

Figure 16.1 – What happens on 1st June 2025

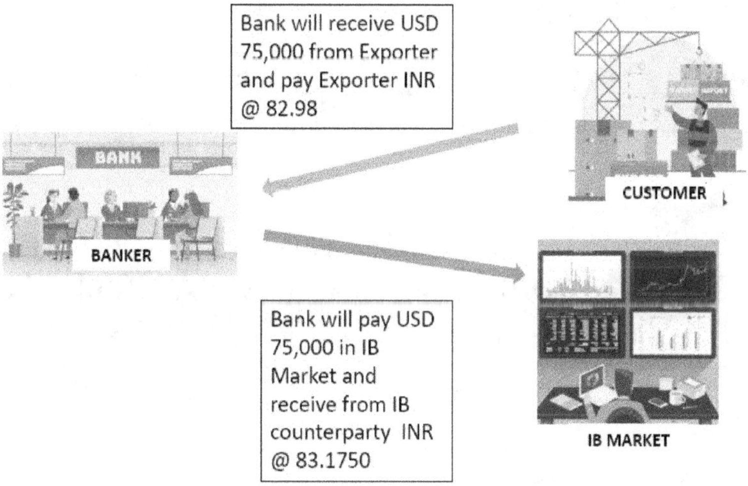

Figure 16.2 – What is expected to happen in October 2025 (Between 1st and 31st October)

b. On 19/8/2025

The customer requests the bank to accept early delivery of the funds under the forward contract.

At this point of time, the following events occur:

a. The bank receives USD 75,000 from the exporter immediately and must provide INR to the exporter at the merchant contracted rate of 82.98. It can do by selling the USD 75,000 in the IB market at the ruling IB spot buying rate, ie., 83.2225.

b. Remember, that in anticipation of receiving USD 75,000 in October, *the Bank had already entered into a forward sale contract, delivery October @ 83.1750.* But now the exporter has delivered the USD 75,000 on 19th August itself and wants INR immediately *(and, therefore, will not be able to deliver the USD in October 2025).*

c. Hence, the bank has a situation in which it has surplus USD 75,000 on 19th August and shortfall of USD 75,000 in October, 2025.

d. In order to set this position right, the bank would enter into a *swap transaction* in the interbank market. Under the swap transaction, would simultaneously sell USD 75,000 spot and buy USD 75,000 maturity October 2025 (called a Sell-Buy swap).

What is a Swap transaction?

A swap transaction is one where there is a simultaneous purchase and sale of a certain foreign currency. There are, therefore, two legs in a swap – the first leg involving purchase or sale of a foreign currency; and a second leg involving the sale and purchase of that currency.

The tenor of the two legs is different. For example, the first leg can be spot and the second leg can be forward, or vice versa. Both the legs may also be forward, but for different periods – say first leg sale 1 month forward, and second leg purchase 3 months forward.

When the purchase leg is the first leg, the swap is termed as "buy-sell swap" and if the sale leg is the first leg, the swap is called a "sell-buy swap".

Swaps are undertaken in order to eliminate mismatches in flows of currencies.

In the example given above, the first leg is a sale (spot) and the second leg is a purchase (forward). Hence, it is a sell-buy swap.

e. The INR generated from the spot sale would be used to pay the exporter immediately, and the USD now bought with maturity October would be used to offset the USD sold forward in the original IB contract that the bank had entered into, on 1st June 2025.

In this example, what actually happens on 19th August 2025 and its impact on what happens on 31st October 2025, are depicted in the following figures 16.3 and 16.4.

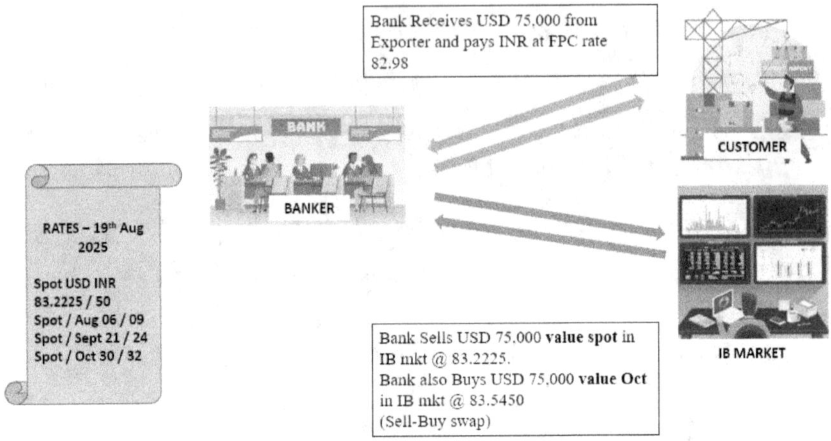

Figure 16.3 What happens on 19th August, 2025

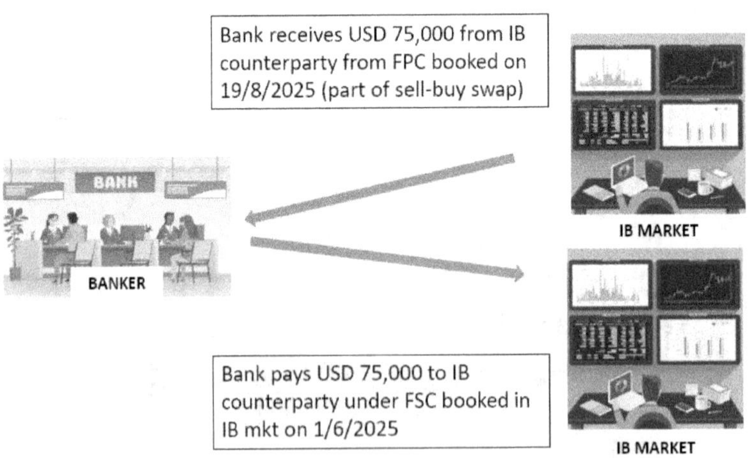

Figure 16.4 – What actually happens on 31st October 2025

The above situation results in two different types of costs. These are:

- Swap cost, and
- Interest on outflow / inflow of funds

I. Swap cost – this is the cost associated with the sell-buy swap and constitutes the difference between the IB spot buying rate and the IB forward selling rate.

[Remember: In the sell-buy swap, the bank sells USD spot at the IB spot buying rate (thereby receiving INR), and buys USD forward, at the IB forward selling rate (thereby paying INR)]

Hence, in this case, the difference is calculated as follows:

IB spot buying rate = 83.2225 (funds **receivable** by the bank)

IB forward selling rate = (83.2250+0.32) = 83.5450 (funds **payable** by the bank)

Difference * = (83.2225 – 83.5450) = (-) 0.3225 (cost to bank, as the difference in negative)

[* difference between the IB spot buying rate and the IB forward selling rate]

Total cost to the bank on the swap deal, therefore, is (75,000 x 0.3225) = INR 24,187.50, or INR 24,188.

This cost, known as swap cost, will have to be recovered from the customer, as part of the charges for early delivery under the forward contract.

The computation of the swap difference of INR 24,188 is depicted in the following figure 16.5.

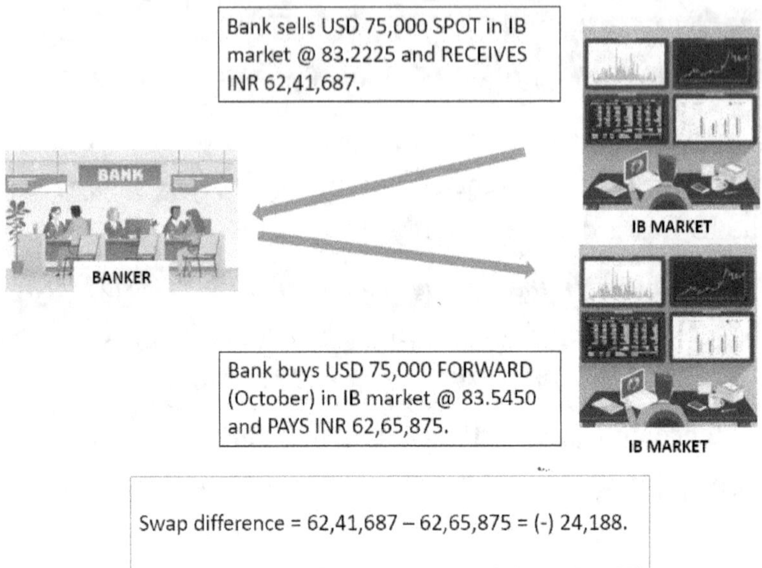

Figure 16.5 Computation of swap difference

[Note: Had the swap difference been positive, there would be a swap gain (instead of swap cost) and the swap gain would be passed on to the customer].

II. *Interest on outflow / inflow of funds* – This constitutes the interest payable / receivable on funds that are, either, laid out (outflow) or flow in (inflow), as a result of the early delivery of the contract.

Explanation:

On 19/8/2025, the bank received USD 75,000 from the exporter, and the same was sold in the interbank market at the IB buying rate of 83.2225.

However, the bank, having accepted early delivery, is obligated to pay the exporter INR at the forward contracted rate of 82.98, irrespective of what the IB buying rate is on 19/8/2025.

Hence, amount received by the bank due to IB sale = 75,000 x 83.2225 = INR 62,41,687.

And the amount paid by the bank to the exporter = 75,000 x 82.98 = INR 62,23,500.

Accordingly, in this case, since the Bank receives more funds than what is pays to the exporter, there is a NET INFLOW of funds = INR 62,41,687 - 62,23,500 = INR 18,187.

The net inflow received will remain with the bank during the period 19/8/2025 to 31/10/2025 (when the transaction will be finally concluded), ie., for a period of 73 days.

The net inflow can, according to the information provided, be invested @ 4% pa.

Therefore, the interest earned by the bank on the net inflow of funds would be (18,187 x (73 / 365) x 4%) = INR 145.

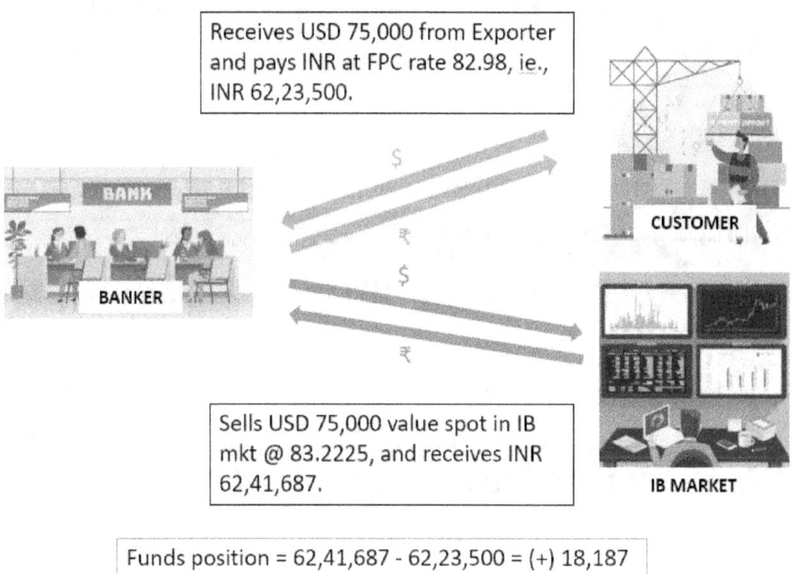

Figure 16.6 Computation of inflow / outflow of funds

Therefore, the total profit or loss to the bank by accepting early delivery of funds =

Swap difference		- 24,188
Interest on outlay of funds	+	145
Total	**-**	**24,043**

Since there is an overall loss of INR 24,043 incurred by the bank, the same would be recovered by the bank from the exporter, as **early delivery charges**.

Had the situation been otherwise, and had the bank booked a profit by accepting the early delivery of funds, the bank would pass on the profit amount to the exporter.

SUMMING UP THE MECHANISM:

Having understood the mechanism involved in early delivery under a forward contract, we can simplify the example and compute the costs as follows:

I. Swap difference:

Amount to be RECEIVED by bank (IB spot buying rate) = 75,000 x 83.2225 = INR 62,41,687.

Amount to be PAID by bank (IB October selling rate) = 75,000 x 83.5450 = INR 62,65,875.

Swap difference = INR (62,41,687 - 62,65,875) = (-) INR 24,188.

II. Interest payable or receivable by the Bank:

Amount to be RECEIVED by bank (IB spot buying rate) = 75,000 x 83.2225 = INR 62,41,687

Amount to be PAID by bank to the exporter under forward contract = 75,000 x 82.98 = INR 62,23,500

Net inflow = INR 62,41,687 - 62,23,500 = INR 18,187.

Interest earned by the bank on the net inflow of funds for 73 days @ 4% pa = INR 145.

Total charges payable by exporter = (- 24,188 + 149) = INR 24,043.

In case the transaction was one of forward sale of USD to the customer (say, an importer or for an outward remittance customer), the change would be as under:

Swap difference would be difference between the IB forward buying rate and the IB spot selling rate, both rates being as on the date of early delivery, and, While calculating interest on funds flow, the net inflow or net outflow would be based on the difference between the merchant forward contract selling rate and the IB spot selling rate ruling on the date of early delivery.

16.3 RULES FOR EARLY DELIVERY

Keeping the above mechanism in mind, the following two rules can be developed for computation of charges related to early delivery under forward purchase contracts and forward sale contracts.

Rule 16.1 – Early Delivery under Forward Purchase Contract

a. **Swap charges** = Amount x (interbank spot buying rate – interbank forward selling rate on date of early delivery)

   Negative answer denotes charges to be recovered by bank; positive answer denotes charges payable by bank.

b. **Interest of outlay of funds** = {(Amount x interbank spot buying rate on date of early delivery) – (Amount x Forward purchase contract rate given to customer)}

If answer is positive, then there is net inflow of funds to the bank and, interest = net inflow x no. of days (from early delivery date to final maturity date) x rate of interest of inflow of funds.

If answer is negative, then there is net outflow of funds to the bank and, interest = net outflow x no. of days (from early delivery date to final maturity date) x rate of interest of outflow of funds.

Rule 16.2 – Early Delivery under Forward Sale Contract

a. Swap charges = Amount x (interbank forward buying rate - interbank spot selling rate on date of early delivery)

   Negative answer denotes charges to be recovered by bank; positive answer denotes charges payable by bank.

b. Interest of outlay of funds = {(Amount x Forward selling contract rate given to customer) – (Amount x interbank spot selling rate on date of early delivery)}

   If answer is positive, then there is net inflow of funds to the bank and, interest = net inflow x no. of days (from early delivery date to final maturity date) x rate of interest of inflow of funds.

   If answer is negative, then there is net outflow of funds to the bank and, interest = net outflow x no. of days (from early delivery date to final maturity date) x rate of interest of outflow of funds.

Check Your Understanding

16.1

On 7th February, 2025, Ajit Industries, a medium scale manufacturing unit, had entered into a tie-up with Cornish GMBH, for a strategic investment (FDI), in which the German company was to remit an amount of USD 1 million amount by 30th June 2025. In order to hedge itself against any currency fluctuations, Ajit Industries book a forward purchase contract for the said amount on 7/2/2025.

However, due to changing priorities, Cornish requested Ajit Industries to fast-forward the expansion and showed their inclination to remit the funds in April 20225 itself. As such, the inward remittance of USD 1,000,000 on 7th April.

Accordingly, on 8th April, Ajit Industries requested its bankers to accept early delivery of the funds in question, indicating their agreement to bear the charges arising from the early delivery.

What is the amount that will have to be paid by the Ajit Industries?

The USD INR exchange rates were are follows:

On 7/2/2025

Spot USD INR
85.7050 / 7075
Spot / Feb 21 / 23
Spot / Mar 39 / 41
Spot / Apr 46 / 48
Spot / May 56 / 59
Spot / June 65 / 67

On 8/4/2025

Spot USD INR
85.5000 / 5025
Spot / Apr 15 / 12
Spot / May 22 / 25
Spot / June 33 / 35

Exchange margin: 0.15% of purchases and 0.20% on sales

Interest on inflow of funds: 3% pa

Interest on outlay of funds: 7% pa

WORKING

Situation on 7/2/2025, when forward contract booked by exporter.

Forward rate = (85.7050 + 0.5600) – 0.15% = 86.2650 – 0.15% = 86.2650 – 0.1294 = 86.1356 = **86.13**

Situation as on 8/4/2025, when early delivery is requested by the company:

i. Swap difference:

Amount to be received by bank (IB spot buying rate) = 1,000,000 x 85.5000 = INR 8,55,00,000.

Amount to be paid by bank (IB June selling rate) = 1,000,000 x ([85.5025 + 0.3500] = 1,000,000 x 85.8525 = INR 8,58,52,500.

Swap difference = INR (8,55,00,000 - 8,58,52,500) = (-) INR 3,52,500.

ii. Interest on funds flow:

Amount to be paid to the exporter under forward contract = 1,000,000 x 86.13 = INR 8,61,30,000

Amount to be received by bank (IB spot buying rate) = 1,000,000 x 85.5000 = INR 8,55,00,000

Net funds flow = INR 8,55,00,000 - 8,61,30,000 = (-) INR 6,30,000, **ie., net outflow.**

Interest paid by the bank on the net outflow of funds for 83 days (8th April to 30th June) @ 7% pa = **INR 10,028.**

Total charges payable by exporter for early delivery = (3,52,500 + 10,028) = **INR 3,62,528.**

Check Your Understanding

16.2

Sunil Bose, who has obtained admission to New Jersey University in USA, is required to remit fees amounting to USD 60,000 by 30th June 2025. Fearing that the Indian Rupee will depreciate, on 7th February he requests his bankers to book a suitable forward contract.

However, on 3rd April, Sunil receives an email from the University requesting him to remit the amount in a week's time due to certain change in their policy and US immigration guidelines.

On 8th April, therefore, Sunil requests his bank to permit him to utilise the forward contract, booked for June 2025, immediately and that he is willing to bear the charges, if any, for early utilisation of the forward contract.

Using the same exchange rates provided in the last example, calculate the charges that will have to paid by Sunil to his bank.

Situation on 7/2/2025, when forward contract booked by Sunil.

Forward rate = (85.7075 + 0.6700) + 0.20% = 86.3775 + 0.20% = 86.3775 + 0.1728 = 86.5503 = **86.56**

Situation as on 8/4/2025, when early utilisation is requested by Sunil:

i. Swap difference:

Amount to be received by bank (IB June buying rate) = 60,000 x ([85.5000 + 0.3300] = 60,000 x 85.8300 = INR 51,49,800

Amount to be paid by bank (IB spot selling rate) = 60,000 x 85.5025 = INR 51,30,150.

Swap difference = INR (51,49,800 - 51,30,150) = (+) **INR 19,650.**

ii. Interest payable or receivable:

Amount to be received from Sunil under forward contract = 60,000 x 86.56 = INR 51,93,600

Amount to be paid by bank (IB spot selling rate) = 60,000 x 85.5025 = INR 51,30,150

Net inflow = INR 51,93,600- 51,30,150 = (+) **INR 63,450**.

Interest receivable by the bank on the net inflow of funds for 83 days (8th April to 30th June) @ 3% pa = **INR 433.**

Total amount payable by the bank to Sunil for early delivery = (19,650 + 433) = **INR 20,083.**

EXERCISE 16

1. Delta and Sons were expecting to make an import payment amounting to USD 25,000- in April 2026. As such, on 18th December, 2025, they booked a forward contract for the remittance.

   However, on 16th January, 2026, they requested their bank for early delivery under the forward contract, as they wanted to expedite the payment.

   The exchange rates prevailing on 18th December and 16th January were as follows.

18/12/2025	**16/1/2026**
Spot USD INR	Spot USD INR
90.2700 / 25	90.5175 / 5200
Spot / Dec 08 /10	Spot / Jan 12 / 13
Spot / Jan 18 / 19	Spot / Feb 22 / 24
Spot / Feb 29 / 31	Spot / Mar 32 / 34
Spot / Mar 52 / 54	Spot / Apr 49 / 51
Spot / Apr 62 / 64	Spot / May 60/ 62
Spot / May 56 / 59	Spot / June 75 / 76
Spot / June 65 / 67	

Assuming that:

- The bank keeps exchange margin of 0.10% on purchase and 0.20% on sales,
- Interest on funds inflow and outflows are at 4% and 8% pa,

Calculate the charges involved in early delivery of the forward contract.

2. Assuming the same exchange rates and other parameters as in the preceding exercise, if the situation was for Alpha Exports, involving booking of forward contract on 18th December 2025 for covering expected receipt of export proceeds in April 2026, followed by early delivery on 16th January, 2026, calculate the charges for early delivery.

3. Harish Exports submitted an export bill for EUR 35,500- on 8th October 2025, payable during the month of December, 2025.

   The exporters requested their bankers to send the same on collection basis and pay them only on receipt of funds.

   In order to hedge themselves against exchange risk, they booked a forward contract for the same.

   However, the buyers remitted the proceeds of the bill on 4th November 2025 and, as such, the exporters requested their bank for accepting early delivery under the forward contract.

   The exchange rates prevailing on 8th October and 4th November were as follows:

8/10/2025	**4/11/2025**
Spot EUR INR	Spot EUR INR
103.0520 / 0535	103.2552 / 2566
Spot / November	Spot / November
103.9544 / 9583	103.7644 / 103.7698
Spot / December	Spot / December
104.3356 / 3398	104.0548 / 104.0582

Assuming that:

- The bank keeps exchange margin of 0.15% on purchase and 0.25% on sales,
- Interest on funds inflow and outflows are at 4% and 8% pa

Calculate the charges involved in early delivery of the forward contract.

4. Jackson Imports was expecting to make an advance payment of HKD 45,000 in May, 2026. As such, looking at the weakening trend of the INR, they requested their bank, on 8th Jan 2026 to book a forward contract.

   However, their suppliers offered Jackson an attractive discount if they could accelerate the payment and, therefore, on 11th March 2026, the importers instructed their bank to send the remittance, thereby requesting early delivery under the forward contract.

The exchange rates and forward margins on 8th Jan and 11th March were as follows:

8/1/2026	**11/3/2026**
Spot USD INR	Spot USD INR
89.8675 / 89.8700	92.2300 / 25
Spot / Jan 20 / 22	Spot / Mar 23 / 24
Spot / Feb 35 / 37	Spot / Apr 32 / 35
Spot / Mar 49 / 51	Spot / May 47 / 50
Spot / Apr 59 / 60	
Spot / May 72 / 74	
Spot USD HKD	Spot USD HKD
7.7860 / 65	7.8237 / 41
Spot / Jan 101.76 / 93.01	Spot / Mar 110.65 / 103.67
Spot / Feb 153.87 / 150.87	Spot / Apr 135.66 / 132.66
Spot / Mar 275.91 / 272. 91	Spot / May 212.78 / 209.78
Spot / Apr 378.68 / 275.68	
Spot / May 464.85 / 444.85	

Assuming that:

- The bank keeps exchange margin of 0.15% on purchase and 0.25% on sales,
- Interest on funds inflow and outflows are at 4% and 8% pa.

Calculate the charges involved in early delivery of the forward contract.

Chapter 17

Cancellation

17.1 WHAT IS CANCELLATION OF FORWARD CONTRACT

A cancellation of a forward contract is one where the customer does not want to, or is not able to, deliver the foreign currency that had been contracted for, and therefore requests the bank to cancel the forward contract.

Cancellation can be requested for, either on due date of the contract or any date prior to the due date.

17.2 CANCELLATION ON DUE DATE

Rule 17.1:

If forward contract is cancelled *on due date*:

For a forward purchase contract, the contract is cancelled at the ruling TT selling rate and the difference between the contracted forward buying rate and the ruling TT selling rate is recovered from the customer, if there is a loss, or paid to the customer if there is a profit.

For a forward sale contract, the contract is cancelled at the ruling TT buying rate and the difference between the contracted forward selling rate and the ruling TT buying rate is recovered from the customer, if there is a loss, or paid to the customer if there is a profit.

Rationale of the Rule

If you recall from the last section, when a customer books a forward purchase contract with the bank, in order to cover its position, the bank simultaneously books a forward sale contract, for the same maturity, in the interbank market.

As the customer is now no longer able to provide the foreign currency, the bank will have to buy the currency from the interbank market (at the prevalent interbank selling rate) in order to honour the forward sale contract, it had booked earlier on.

Hence, the forward purchase contract is reversed at the ruling selling rate and amount recovered from the customer, after loading suitable exchange margin (ie., TT selling rate). However, having originally booked the forward purchase contract, the customer is entitled to receive the INR equivalent at the forward purchase contract rate.

Therefore, it is only the net difference (between the TT selling rate and forward purchase contract rate) that will be required to recovered from the customer (if there is a loss) or paid to the customer (if there is a profit).

Example:

On 1/1/2025, Omni Exports requests its bankers to book a forward purchase contract for USD 50,000, delivery March 2025, as it is expecting to receive proceeds of an export bill during March.

However, on 31st March, the exporter realises that payment of the bill has run into difficulties due to bankruptcy of the importer, and therefore requests its bank to cancel the contract.

The USD INR rates prevailing, are as follows:

1/1/2025

Spot 85.4550 / 75

Spot / January 12 / 15

Spot / February 28 / 31

Spot / March 41 / 43

Spot / April 50 / 52

31/3/2025

Spot 85.7200 / 25

Spot / April 20 / 23

If the bank levies exchange margin of 0.10% on purchases and 0.15% on sales, what is the amount recoverable / payable to the exporter on cancellation of the contract?

WORKING:

1/1/2025 – booking of forward purchase contract, maturity March 2025:

(85.4550 + 0.2800) – 0.10% = 85.7350 – 0.0857 = 85.6493, or **85.64**

[The bank, simultaneously covers its position by booking a forward sale (delivery March) contract at the ruling interbank forward buying rate, ie. 85.4550 + 0.41 = 85.8650]

31/3/2025 – cancellation of forward purchase contract:

TT selling rate = 85.7225 + 0.15% = 85.7225 + 0.1286 = 85.8511, or **85.86**

Amount payable to exporter at forward purchase rate (50,000 x 85.64)	+ 42,82,000
Amount recoverable from exporter at TT selling rate (50,000 x 85.86)	- (42,93,000)
Net recoverable	11,000

The flow of events involved in booking of the forward contract, followed by its cancellation on due date, are depicted in the following figures.

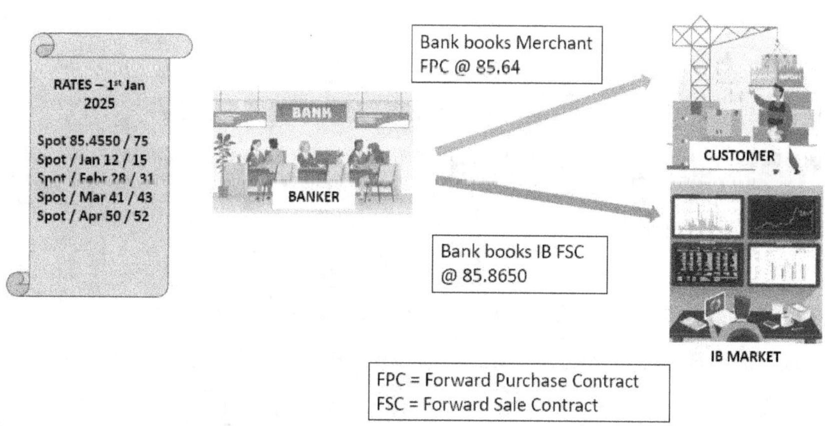

Figure 17.1 What happened on 1/1/2025

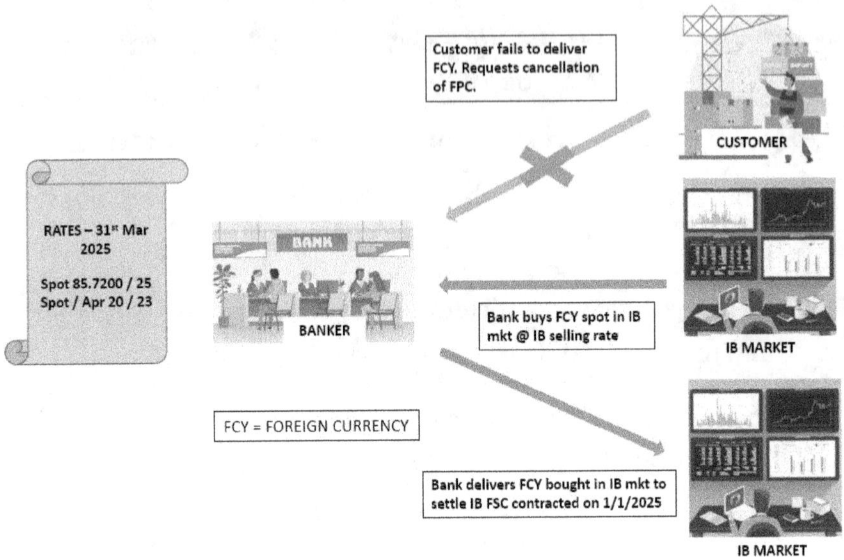

Figure 17.2 What happened on 31/3/2025

If the above example involved booking of a forward sale contract (say, for an importer customer) which is cancelled on due date, the working will be similar in basic concept, the difference being that the importer will be charged / paid the difference between the amount debited at originally booked forward sale contract rate and credited at TT buying rate on date of cancellation.

Example

On 1/1/2025, Meadow Imports requests its bankers to book a forward sale contract for USD 75,000, delivery March 2025, as it is expecting to make payment of an import bill during March.

However, on 31st March, the importer realised the contract had been booked by error as the payment of the import bill was to be adjusted against export proceeds receivable from the same foreign party. The firm, therefore, has requested its bank to cancel the forward contract.

The USD INR rates prevailing, are as follows:

1/1/2025
Spot 85.4550 / 75
Spot / January 12 / 15
Spot / February 28 / 31
Spot / March 41 / 43
Spot / April 50 / 52
31/3/2025
Spot 85.7200 / 25
Spot / April 20 / 23

If the bank charges exchange margin of 0.10% on purchases and 0.15% on sales, what is the amount recoverable / payable to the exporter on cancellation of the contract?

WORKING:

1/1/2025 – booking of forward sale contract. Maturity March 2025:

(85.4575 + 0.4300) + 0.15% = 85.8875 + 0.1288 = 86.0163, or **86.02**

[The bank, simultaneously covers its position by booking a forward purchase (delivery March) contract at the ruling interbank forward selling rate, ie. 85.4575 + 0.43 = 85.8875]

31/3/2025 – cancellation of the forward sale contract:

TT buying rate = 85.7200 - 0.10% = 85.7200 - 0.0858 = 85.6342, or **85.63**

Amount recoverable from importer at forward sale rate (75,000 x 86.02)	(64,51,500)
Amount payable to importer at TT buying rate (75,000 x 85.63)	+ 64,22,250
Net recoverable	29,250

17.3 CANCELLATION PRIOR TO DUE DATE

Rule 17.2:

If cancellation is *prior to due date*:

For a forward purchase contract, the contract is cancelled at the ruling forward selling rate (forward period being that between date of cancellation date and date of original maturity),

and the difference between the contracted forward buying rate and the ruling balance period forward selling rate is recovered from the customer if there is a loss, or paid to the customer if there is a profit.

Similarly,

For a forward sale contract, the contract is cancelled at the ruling forward buying rate (forward period being that between date of cancellation and date of original maturity), and the difference between the contracted forward selling rate and the ruling balance period forward buying rate is recovered from the customer if there is a loss, or paid to the exporter if there is a profit.

Example:

On 1/1/2025, Omni Exports requests its bankers to book a forward purchase contract for USD 50,000, delivery March 2025, as it is expecting to receive proceeds of an export bill during March.

However, on 15th February (ie., before due date of the contract), the exporter realises that payment of the bill has run into difficulties due to bankruptcy of the importer, and therefore requests its bank to cancel the contract.

The USD INR rates prevailing, are as follows:

1/1/2025	**15/2/2025**
Spot 85.4550 / 75	Spot 85.6225 / 50
Spot / January 12 / 15	Spot / February 10 / 13
Spot / February 28 / 31	Spot / March 19 / 22
Spot / March 41 / 43	Spot / April 36 / 38
Spot / April 50 / 52	

If the bank charges exchange margin of 0.10% on purchases and 0.15% on sales, what is the amount recoverable / payable to the exporter on cancellation of the contract on 15/2/2025?

WORKING:

1/1/2025 – booking of forward purchase contract, maturity March 2025:

(85.4550 + 0.2800) – 0.10% = 85.7350 – 0.0857 = 85.6493, or **85.64**

15/2/2025 – cancellation of forward contract:

Forward selling rate (maturity March 2025) = (85.6250 + 0.22) + 0.15% = 85.8450 + 0.1288 = 85.9738, or **85.98**.

Amount payable to exporter at forward purchase rate (50,000 x 85.64)	+ 42,82,000
Amount recoverable from exporter at forward selling rate (for balance period) = (50,000 x 85.98)	- (42,99,000)
Net recoverable	17,000

The flow of events involved in booking of the forward contract, followed by its cancellation prior to its due date, are depicted in the following figures.

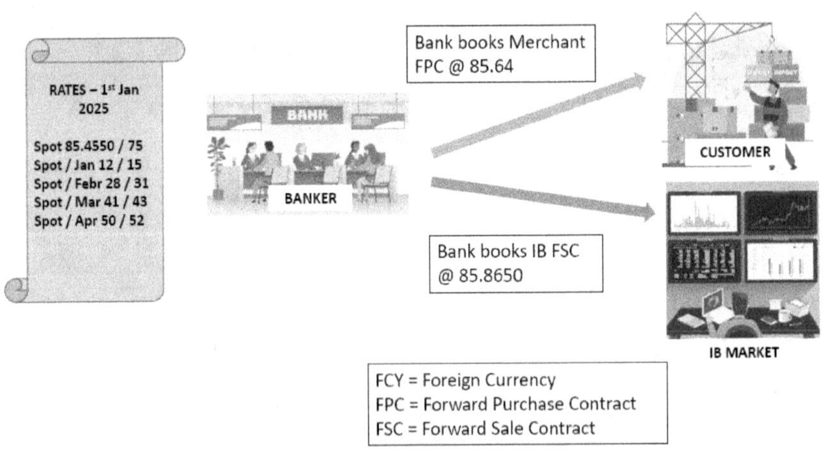

Figure 17.3 What happened on 1/1/2025

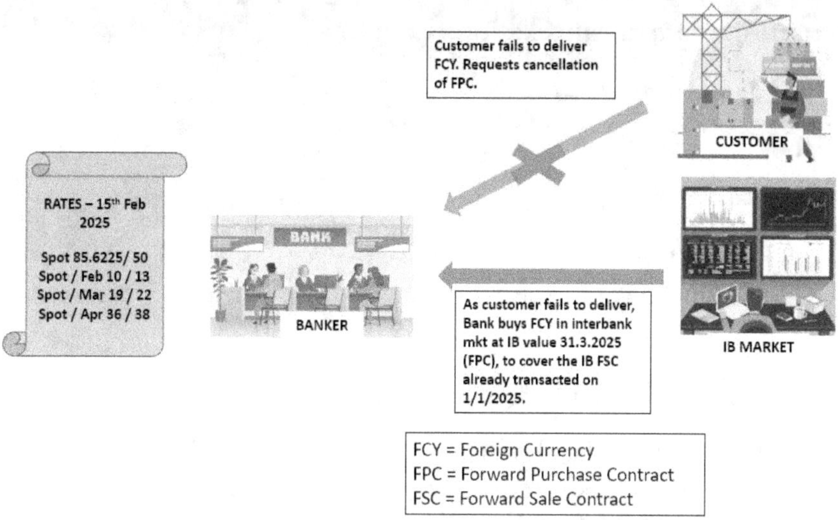

Figure 17.4 What happened on 15/2/2025

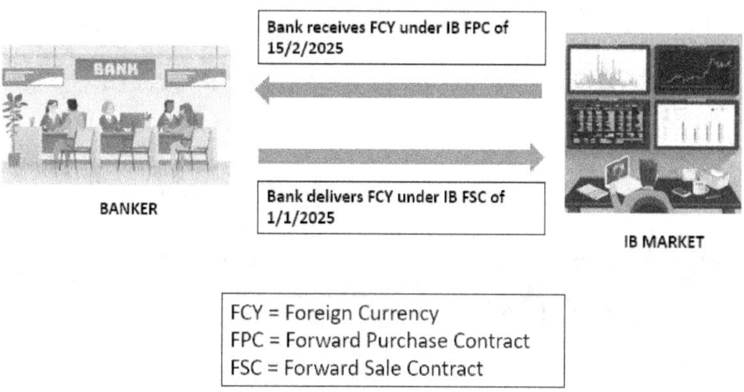

Figure 17.5 What happened on 31/3/2025

If the above example involved booking of a forward sale contract (say, for an importer customer) which is cancelled on due date, the working will be similar in concept, the difference being that the customer will be charged / paid the difference between the amount to be debited at originally booked forward sale contract rate and amount to be credited at the *forward* buying rate (for balance period) on date of cancellation.

Check Your Understanding

17.1

On 15/7/2025, Kaycee Imports requested its bankers to book a forward sale contract for USD 100,000, delivery November 2025, as it was expecting to make an advance payment for materials during November.

However, on 30th November, the importer realised that the order would have to be deferred and, therefore, no advance payment was required to be made. It, therefore requested its bank to cancel the contract.

The USD INR rates prevailing, are as follows:

15/7/2025	**30/11/2025**
Spot 85.9925 / 50	Spot 89.4625 / 50
Spot / July 08 / 11	Spot / December 25 / 28
Spot / August 29 / 31	Spot / January 45 / 48
Spot / September 42 / 45	
Spot / October 55 / 57	
Spot / November 72 / 74	
Spot / December 90 / 92	

If the bank levies exchange margin of 0.15% on purchases and 0.20% on sales, what is the amount recoverable from / payable to the importer on cancellation of the contract?

WORKING:

15/7/2025 – booking of forward sale contract. Maturity November 2025:

(85.9950 + 0.7400) + 0.20% = 86.7350 + 0.1735 = 86.9085, or 86.91

30/11/2025

TT buying rate = 89.4625 - 0.15% = 89.4625 - 0.1342 = 89.3283, or 89.32

Amount recoverable from importer at forward sale rate (100,000 x 86.91)	(-) 86,91,000
Amount payable to importer at TT buying rate (100,000 x 89.32)	+ 89,32,000
Net payable to importer	2,41,000

Check Your Understanding

17.2

On 15/7/2025, Carmel Exports requests its bankers to book a forward purchase contract for USD 25,000, delivery November 2025, as it is expecting to receive proceeds of an export bill during November.

However, on 10th September, the exporter realises that the buyer has filed for bankruptcy, and therefore, requests its bank to cancel the contract.

The USD INR rates prevailing, are as follows:

15/7/2025	**10/9/2025**
Spot 85.9925 / 50	Spot 88.0500 / 25
Spot / July 08 / 11	Spot / September 21 / 24
Spot / August 29 / 31	Spot / October 31 / 35
Spot / September 42 / 45	Spot / November 45 / 48
Spot / October 55 / 57	Spot / December 60 / 62
Spot / November 72 / 74	Spot / January 70 / 71
Spot / December 90 / 92	

If the bank charges exchange margin of 0.10% on purchases and 0.15% on sales, what is the amount recoverable / payable to the exporter on cancellation of the contract?

WORKING:

15/7/2025 – booking of forward purchase contract. Maturity November 2025:

(85.9925 + 0.5500) – 0.10% = 86.5425 – 0.0865 = 86.4560, or 86.45

10/9/2025

Forward selling rate (maturity November 2025) = (88.0525 + 0.4800) + 0.15% = 88.5325 + 0.1328 = 88.6653, or 88.67

Amount payable to exporter at forward purchase rate (25,000 x 86.45)	+ 21,61,250
Amount recoverable from exporter at forward selling rate (for balance period) = (25,000 x 88.67)	- (22,16,750)
Net recoverable from exporter	55,500

EXERCISE 17

1. On 4th February, 2026, Gala Exports booked a forward contract delivery for EUR 75,000 delivery April 2026, towards expected advance remittance to be received from a buyer in the Germany.

   However unfortunately, due to the war in West Asia, the buyers changed their plans and, on 14th March, they advised that they would be delaying the remittance indefinitely. Accordingly, Gala Exports requested their bank to cancel the forward contract.

   Given the following prevailing exchange rates and forward margins, calculate the forward contract cancellation charges.

4/2/2026	**14/3/2026**
Spot USD INR 90.4250 / 75	Spot USD INR 92.5800 / 25
Spot / Feb 12 / 15	Spot / Mar 20 / 22
Spot / Mar 22 / 23	Spot / Apr 41 /43
Spot / Apr 31 / 34	
Spot EUR USD 1.1334 / 36	Spot EUR USD 1.1514 / 16
Spot / Feb 11.68 / 11.96	Spot / Mar 12.22 / 12.56
Spot / Mar 17.29 / 17.59	Spot / Apr 21.78 / 21.90
Spot / Apr 32.78 / 33.16	

   Assume that the bank levies exchange margin of 0.20% and 0.25% on its purchases and sales.

2. Mayfair Industries, which is in the business of manufacturing paints, imports resins from Canada. Expecting to make an advance remittance of CAD 22,000 during April 2026, on 15th Dec 2025 it booked a forward contract.

   However, due to disruptions resulting from the West Asia conflict, its productions suffered and the Company had to put its future production plans on hold. Accordingly, on 3rd March 2026, it requested its bank to cancel the forward contract.

   Given the following prevailing exchange rates and forward margins, calculate the forward contract cancellation charges.

15/12/2025	3/3/2026
Spot USD INR 90.6550 / 75	Spot USD INR 91.5625 / 50
Spot / Dec 14 / 15	Spot / Mar 20 / 22
Spot / Jan 28 / 30	Spot / Apr 41 / 43
Spot / Feb 37 / 39	
Spot / Mar 48 / 50	Spot USD CAD 1.4483 / 4502
Spot / Apr 60 / 61	Spot / Mar 11.05 / 10.90
	Spot / Apr 21.55 / 21.35
Spot USD CAD 1.3770 / 3782	
Spot / Dec 8.49 / 8.27	
Spot / Jan 18.62 / 18.22	
Spot / Feb 36.18 / 35.78	
Spot / Mar 55.95 / 53.95	
Spot / Apr 71.05 / 70.43	

Assume that the bank levies exchange margin of 0.20% and 0.25% on its purchases and sales.

3. Corus Technologies was expecting to remit licence fees amounting to USD 18,000 in February 2026. Accordingly, on 15/12/2025, it booked a forward contract.

   However, due to certain disputes, the payment was held up and on 28/2/2026, the bank cancelled the forward contract.

   Given the following prevailing exchange rates and forward margins, calculate the forward contract cancellation charges.

15/12/2025	**28/2/2026**
Spot USD INR 90.6550 / 75	Spot USD INR 91.0800 / 25
Spot / Dec 14 / 15	Spot / Mar 12 / 13
Spot / Jan 28 / 30	
Spot / Feb 37 / 39	
Spot / Mar 48 / 50	

   Assume that the bank levies exchange margin of 0.10% and 0.20% on its purchases and sales.

4. Govind Exports submitted a bill for AUD 52,000 to its bankers on 15/12/2025, with a request to send the same for payment on collection basis. The bill was payable at 45 days after sight and, accordingly, the exporter booked a forward contract with its bank for delivery in February 2026.

However, since the proceeds of the bill were delayed, on 28/2/2026, the exporters requested the bank to cancel the forward contract.

Given the following prevailing exchange rates and forward margins, calculate the forward contract cancellation charges.

15/12/2025	**28/2/2026**
Spot USD INR 90.6550 / 75	Spot USD INR 90.6550 / 75
Spot / Dec 14 / 15	Spot / Dec 14 / 15
Spot / Jan 28 / 30	Spot / Jan 28 / 30
Spot / Feb 37 / 39	Spot / Feb 37 / 39
Spot / Mar 48 / 50	Spot / Mar 48 / 50
Spot AUD USD 0.6955 / 65	Spot AUD USD 0.7112 / 20
Spot / Dec 1.19 / 1.11	Spot / Mar 2.8 / 2.5
Spot / Jan 2.6 / 2.5	
Spot / Feb 5.7 / 5.5	
Spot / Mar 9.7 / 9.3	

Assume that the bank levies exchange margin of 0.15% and 0.25% on its purchases and sales.

Chapter 18

Extension

18.1 WHAT IS EXTENSION OF FORWARD CONTRACT

Extension of a forward contract is one where the customer requests for deferment of the option period, or deferment of the fixed maturity / expiry date.

For example, an exporter, on 1/1/2026 booked a forward purchase contract with delivery period February 2026. However, on 29th January, the exporter request to extend the delivery period to April 2026.

Or, say, an exporter, on 1/1/2026, booked a forward purchase contract with fixed maturity date 27th February 2026. However, on the maturity date (27/2/2026), the exporter has requested to extend the maturity date to 30th to April 2026.

Any request for extension of a forward contract must be made before the original forward contract expires. Extensions cannot, therefore, be requested for once the original contract has expired.

18.2 HOW IS A FORWARD CONTRACT EXTENDED?

A forward contract is extended by, first, cancelling the original contract and simultaneously booking a fresh contract for the extended period.

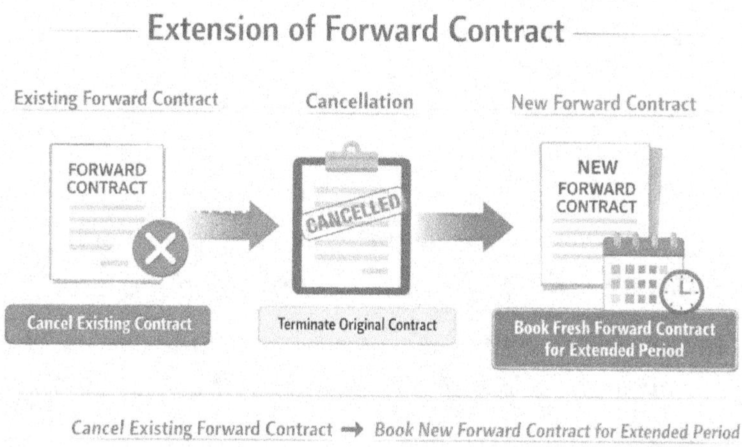

Figure 18.1 Mechanism of extension of forward contract

Example:

India Exports, on 1/1/2025, in anticipation of receipt of export proceeds amounting to USD 250,000 had booked a USD INR forward contract, delivery March 2025 @ 85.64.

However, on 30/3/2025, the foreign buyer informed India Exports that there would be a delay of 2 months, owing to certain financial difficulties it was facing.

Therefore, on 31/3/2025, the exporter requested its bankers to extend the forward contract by further two months, ie., till end of May 2025.

Extension of forward contract, as requested here, involves two steps, viz.,

Step 1 – cancellation of the original forward contract, at the forward selling rate ruling on 31/3/2025 (for the unexpired period of the original contract), , and

Step 2 – booking a fresh forward purchase contract, at rates ruling on 31/3/2025.

[Note: Since normally requests for extensions are received before the maturity date of the original contract, the rate applicable in Step 1 will be the forward selling rate for the unexpired period.

However, in case the request is received on the maturity date of the original contract, then the applicable rate in Step 1 will be the ruling TT selling rate.

This principle is the same as what rules when forward contracts are cancelled and covered in chapter 17].

The charges involved in cancellation of the original forward contract will be recovered / paid to the customer depending upon whether there was a loss or profit while cancelling the forward contract.

In the above example, let us presume that the USD INR exchange rates prevailing on 31st March 2025 were as follows, and the bank levied exchange margin of 0.10% on purchases and 0.15% on sales.

31/3/2025
Spot 85.7200 / 25
Spot / April 20 / 23
Spot / May 46 / 48
Spot / June 55 / 58

WORKING:

1. Cancellation of forward contract on 31/3/2025:

   [Since the request for extension was received on the maturity date of the original contract – 31/3/2025, the applicable rate for cancellation will be the ruling TT selling rate.]

   TT selling rate = 85.7225 + 0.15% = 85.7225 + 0.1286 = 85.85.

Amount payable to exporter at forward purchase rate (250,000 x 85.64)	+ 2,14,10,000
Amount recoverable from exporter at TT selling rate (250,000 x 85.85)	- (2,14,62,500)
Net recoverable	**52,500**

Booking of fresh forward purchase contract:

Forward purchase contract rate (available during May 2025) = (85.7200 + 0.20) – 0.10%

= 85.9200 – 0.0859 = 85.8341, or **85.83.**

Hence, extension of the forward contract involves recovery of extension charges of INR 52,500 and booking the fresh contract, valid during May 2025, at 85.83.

Check Your Understanding

18.1

Delta Industries had, on 23rd June 2025, contracted with Gomez, Inc, USA to import a furnace at a landed cost of USD 750,000. It had expected to receive the furnace during the month of September 2025. Accordingly, it booked a forward contract with its bank on that day to cover the import transaction.

However, on 18th July, the exporter in US advised that due to production disruption at their factory, the shipment was delayed and expected to be received only in December, 2025.

Accordingly, on 21st July, the representative of Delta Industries requested the bank to extend the forward contract till December 2025.

What will be the extension charges that the importer will need to pay its bankers and at what revised rate would the forward contract be extended, if the bank levies exchange margin of 0.15% on purchase and sales transactions?

The USD INR rates on 23rd June and 21st July were as follows:

23/6/2025	21/7/2025
Spot 86.7950 / 75	Spot 86.3300 / 25
Spot / June 12 / 15	Spot / August 07 / 09
Spot / July 26 / 28	Spot / September 15 / 18
Spot / August 39 / 42	Spot / October 30 / 33
Spot / September 50 / 52	Spot / November 52 / 55
Spot / October 70 / 72	Spot / December 71 / 74
Spot / January 85 / 87	Spot / January 85 / 87

WORKING:

On 23/6.2025

Forward sale contract booked, delivery September - (86.7975 + 0.52) + 0.15%

= 87.3175 + 0.15% = 87.3175 + 0.1310 = 87.4485, or 87.45.

On 21/7/2025

Forward (Sept) Buying rate = (86.3300 + 0.15) - 0.15% = 86.4800 – 0.1297 = 86.3503

[Since the request for extension was received before the maturity date of the original contract – 30/9/2025, the applicable rate for cancellation will be the ruling forward (September) buying rate.]

Amount recoverable from importer at forward sale contract rate (750,000 x 87.45)	6,55,87,500
Amount payable to importer at TT buying rate (750,000 x 86.3503)	6,47,62,725
Net recoverable from importer	**8,24,775**

[Note: The forward buying rate, in this calculation, has not been rounded off to 2 decimal places, since this is only an intermediate rate being used to determine charges for cancellation of the contract and this rate is not actually being quoted to the customer.]

Fresh forward sale contract booking, delivery December 2025 = (86.3325 + 0.74) + 0.15%

= 87.0725 + 0.15% = 87.0725 + 0.1306 = 87.2031, or **87.21**

Hence, extension of the forward contract involves recovery of extension charges of INR 8,24,775 and booking the fresh contract, valid during December 2025 at 87.21.

Check Your Understanding

18.2

Colby Steel Manufacturing Co Ltd entered into an MOU with Cogen Inc in USA, in January 2025, for setting up a unit for manufacture of green steel. Towards this project, Cogen Inc had agreed to invest USD 500,000 in Colby Steels by May 2025.

Accordingly, Colby Steels booked a forward purchase contract, on 10th January 2025 to cover the expected investment, with the forward contract being available during May 2025.

However, due to unforeseen events, Cogen Inc, on 4th April advised Colby Steels that their investment would be delayed for two months and would, therefore, be expected only in July 2025.

Colby Inc, therefore, on 7th April requested its bankers to extend the forward contract so as to make it available during July 2025.

What would be the amount of extension charges payable by Colby Steels and what would be the revised forward contract rate, if the bank levies exchange margin of 0.10% on purchases and 0.15% on sales transactions?

The USD INR rates on 10th January and 7th April were as follows:

10/1/2025	7/4/2025
Spot 86.0150 / 75	Spot 85.8200 / 25
Spot / Jan 15 / 17	Spot / Apr 20 / 22
Spot / Feb 25 / 28	Spot / May 30 / 33
Spot / Mar 40 / 42	Spot / June 48 / 50
Spot / Apr 55 / 58	Spot / July 66 / 68
Spot / May 70 / 72	Spot / Aug 78 / 81
Spot / June 83 / 85	
Spot / July 99 / 102	
Spot / Aug 120 / 122	

WORKING:

On 10/1/2025

Booking of forward purchase contract, delivery May 2025 = (86.0150 + 0.55) – 0.10%

= 86.5650 – 0.10% = 86.1525 – 0.0866 = 86.4784, or 86.47

On 7/4/2025

Forward (May) selling rate = (85.8225 + 0.33) + 0.15% = 86.1525 + 0.15% = 86.1525 + 0.1292 = 86.2817.

Amount payable to Colby Steels at forward purchase contract rate (500,000 x 86.47)	4,32,35,000
Amount recoverable from Colby Steels at TT selling rate (500,000 x 86.2817)	4,31,40,850
Net payable to Colby Steels	94,150

Fresh forward purchase contract booking, delivery July 2025 = (85.8200 + 0.48) – 0.10% =

= 86.3000 – 0.10% = 86.3000 – 0.0863 = 86.2137, or, **86.21**

Hence, extension of the forward contract involves payment of extension charges of INR 94,150 to Colby Steels and booking the fresh contract, valid during July 2025 at 86.21.

EXERCISE 18

1. On 1/1/2026, Greaves Industries booked a forward contract, delivery February 2026, in anticipation of payment of an import bill amounting to USD 25,000.

   However, due to labour unrest at their plant, operations were disrupted and cash flows affected.

   Accordingly, on 27th Feb, 2026 (28th Feb being a holiday), the company requested its bankers to extend the contract for 2 months.

   Calculate the extension charges and fresh contract rate, given the following exchange rates.

1/1/2026	**27/2/2025**
USD INR Spot 90.0200 / 25	USD INR Spot 91.1050 / 75
Spot / Jan 15 / 17	Spot / Mar 18 / 20
Spot / Feb 25 / 28	Spot / Apr 29 / 32
Spot / Mar 40 / 42	Spot / May 44 / 46

   Assume that the bank retains exchange margin of 0.10% and 0.15% on purchases and sales, respectively.

2. Omega Exports submitted documents to its bankers on 21/11/2025 amounting to USD 35,000-. The documents were drawn at 60 days after sight and the company requested its bankers to send the same on collection basis.

In order to mitigate exchange risk, the exporter requested the bank to book a forward contract with delivery during January 2026.

However, there was a delay in payment by the buyers and, accordingly, on 31/1/2026, Omega Exports requested the bank to extend the contract up to March 2026.

Calculate the extension charges and fresh contract rate, given the following exchange rates.

21/11/2025	**31/1/2026**
USD INR Spot 89.6275 / 6300	USD INR Spot 91.6825 / 50
Spot / Nov 28 / 31	Spot / Jan 13 / 16
Spot / Dec 35 / 36	Spot / Feb 26 / 27
Spot / Jan 56 / 58	Spot Mar 38 / 40
Spot / Feb 69 / 71	Spot Apr 58 / 59

Assume that the bank retains exchange margin of 0.10% and 0.15% on purchases and sales, respectively.

3. Calculate the extension charges for the following forward sale contract, as well as the fresh rate for the extended contract.

   Original contract date: 25/11/2025

   Amount = USD 45,000

   Merchant forward sale contract rate: 92.26

   Maturity date of contract: 31/1/2026

   Extension requested on: 15/12/2025

Extension required for: 1 month

USD INR rates prevailing on 15/12/2025, as follows:

15/12/2025
USD INR Spot 90.7700 / 25
Spot / Dec 21 / 23
Spot / Jan 35 / 36
Spot / Feb 50 / 52
Spot / Mar 61 / 63
Spot / Apr 75 / 78

Bank's levies exchange margin of 0.10% and 0.20% on purchases and sales, respectively.

4. Ajanta Exports was expecting to receive an advance remittance of USD 1,00,000- from a new buyer in December 2025. Accordingly, on 4th November 2025, it booked a forward contract to cover the expected transaction @ 88.80.

   However, the buyer expressed liquidity constraints and advised that there would be delay of 2 months for making the advance payment.

   Hence, on 4th Dec, the exporter requested its bankers to extend the contract for 2 months.

   Calculate the extension charges and fresh contract rate, given the following exchange rates on 4/12/2025.

4/12/2025

USD INR Spot 90.1525 / 50

Spot / Dec 18 / 21

Spot / Jan 34 / 35

Spot / Feb 45 / 46

Spot / Mar 60 / 63

Assume that the bank retains exchange margin of 0.15% and 0.25% on purchases and sales, respectively.

Solutions to Exercises

EXERCISE 2

1. All a, b and c
2. a and b only
3. None of the statements are true
4. b
5. a

EXERCISE 3

1. All a, b and c
2. a and b
3. a
4. b
5. b
6. a

EXERCISE 4

1. c
2. b
3. a
4. b
5. b
6. a
7. c
8. c
9. a

WORKING:

1 GBP = USD 1.4110

1 EUR = USD 1.1850

Or, USD 1 = EUR 1 ÷ 1.1850

Or, USD 1.4110 = EUR 1.4110 ÷ 1.1850 = EUR 1.1907

EUR 1 = GBP 0.9000

Or, EUR 1.1907 = GBP (1.1907 x 0.9000) = GBP 1.0716

Hence, starting from GBP 1, by selling GBP, buying USD, selling USD and buying EUR and, finally, selling EUR and buying GBP, we have come to a result of GBP 1.0716, ie., a profit of (1.0716 – 1.000) = GBP 0.0716.

10. b

WORKING

Sell JPY 144.22 and buy USD 1

Sell USD 1 and buy HKD 7.8200

HKD 1 = JPY 1 ÷ 0.0600 = JPY 16.6667

Sell HKD 7.8200 and buy JPY (7.8200 x 16.6667) = JPY 130.3336

Profit = JPY (130.3336 – 144.2200) = (-) 13.8864

Hence, there is a loss of JPY 13.8864.

EXERCISE 5

1. b	2. b	3. a	4. b
5. a	6. b	7. b	8. b

EXERCISE 6

1. b	2. a	3. b
4. a	5. b	6. a
7. b	8. a	9. b
10. b	11. a	

EXERCISE 7

1. This is a case where the bank will quote its buying rate to the exporter.

   The merchant exchange rate is calculated as follows:

Interbank USD INR rate	90.3250
Deduct profit margin @ 0.20%	0.1807
	90.1443
Merchant USD INR Selling rate	90.14
Amount to be credited to Co's account as equivalent of USD 32,000 @ 90.14	INR 28,84,480

2. This is a case of an outward remittance amounting to USD 5,500-

   The merchant exchange rate is calculated as follows:

Interbank USD INR rate	90.3250
ADD profit margin @ INR 0.10	0.1000
	90.4250
Merchant USD INR Selling rate	90.43

3. This is a case of an outward remittance amounting to USD 55,000-

   The merchant exchange rate is calculated as follows:

Interbank USD INR rate	91.2250
ADD profit margin @ 0.20%	0.1825
	91.4075
Merchant USD INR Selling rate	91.41

4. This is a case of receipt of inward remittance owing to refund of the advance payment made earlier.

   The merchant exchange rate is calculated as follows:

Interbank buying rate	90.8800
LESS profit margin @ INR 0.0750	0.0750
	90.8050
Merchant USD INR Buying Rate	90.80

EXERCISE 8

1. This is a case of indirect quotation in the intermediate transaction (NZD USD)

   NZD INR buying rate = 91.1025 x 0.5811 = **52.9397**

2. This is a case of direct quotation in the intermediate transaction (USD CAD)

   CAD INR selling rate = 91.0000 ÷ 1.3722 = **66.3169**

3. This is a case of direct quotation in the intermediate transaction (USD IDR), with the IDR INR rate expressed in terms of 10,000 IDR.

   IDR INR rate = 90.5550 ÷ 17256 / 90.5575 ÷ 16979

= 0.0052477 / 0.0053335

Or, **10000 IDR = INR 52.48 / 53.34**

4. This is a case of direct quotation in the intermediate transaction (USD SGD) and it is required to calculate the SGD INR buying rate.

   SGD INR buying rate = 90.6250 ÷ 1.2826 = 70.6573 less 0.10%

   = 70.6573 – 0.0707 = 70.5866, ie., **70.58**

5. This is a case of indirect quotation in the intermediate transaction (AUD USD) and it is required to calculate the AUD INR selling rate.

   AUD INR selling rate = 91.2200 x 0.7103 = **64.7936**

6. Amount of credit to the current account of Chemsel Exports Ltd

   = 5,250,333 x 91.2175 = INR 47,89,22,250.43, ie., **INR 47,89,22,250-**

EXERCISE 9

1. a 2. b 3. c 4. d 5. a 6. b

EXERCISE 10

1. c 2. c 3. a 4. c 5. c

EXERCISE 11

1. a 2. b 3. b 4. a 5. b

EXERCISE 12

1. Two-month forward GBP USD rate

   = 1.3396 – (2.2000÷10000) = 1.3396 – 0.0002 = 1.3394

2. Three-month forward AUD USD rate

   = 0.6970 – (9.7÷10000) = 0.6970 – 0.0010 = 0.6960

3. Six-month forward USD CAD rate

   = 1.3792 – (104.72÷10000) = 1.3792 – 0.0105 = 1.3687

4. 12-month forward USD INR rate

   = 93.1025 + (261.5000÷100) = 93.1025 + 2.6150 = 95.7175

5. Three-month forward USD JPY rate

   158.91 – (126.06 ÷ 100) = 158.90 – 1.26 = 157.64

EXERCISE 13

1. This is a case of calculating TT buying rate for USD

   WORKING

   TT Buying rate = 91.2025 – 0.15% = 91.2025 – 0.1368

   = 91.0657, or 91.06

2. This is a case of calculation of TT buying rate for EUR

   WORKING

   EUR INR buying rate = 92.3050 x 1.1467 = 105.8461

   EUR TT buying rate = 105.8461 – 0.25% = 105.8461 – 0.2646

   = 105.5815, or 105.58.

3. This is a case of calculating Bill Buying rate. Since the bill is payable at sight, only NTP of 25 days is involved.

   Accordingly, due date = 12/3/2026 + 25 days = 6th April 2026.

   Forward USD INR buying rate with premium up to March 2026 = 92.2000 + 0.06 = 92.2600

   Bill buying rate = 92.2600 – 0.10% = 92.2600 – 0.0923 = 92.1677. or 92.17

4. This is a case of calculating Bill Buying rate. Since the bill has a fixed due date, no NTP will be added.

   Due date of bill = 4/3/2026 + 90 days = 2nd June 2026.

   Forward USD INR buying rate with premium up to May 2026 = 91.6775 + 0.36 = 92.0375

   Bill buying rate = 92.0375 – 0.15% = 92.0375 – 0.1381

   = 91.8994, or 91.89

5. This is a case of calculating Bill Buying rate for a bill payable 60 days after sight. The total forward period will be NTP + usance period = 25 + 60 = 85 days (ie., less than 3 months).

   Due date of bill = 11/9/2025 + 85 days = 10th November 2025.

   Forward USD INR buying rate with **discount** up to 3rd month = 88.7325 - 0.2900

   = 88.4425

   [Note: since USD INR is at a discount, and the bill is due between 2nd and 3rd months, the discount up to 3rd month will be deducted for calculating the forward rate.]

Bill buying rate = 88.4425 - 0.05% = 88.4425 – 0.0442 = 88.3983, or 88.39.

6. Bill amount = USD 265,000. Margin = 25% USD 66,250.

   Therefore, bill amount to be discounted = USD 265,000 – 66,250 = USD 198,750.

   = INR (198,750 x 88.39) = INR 1,75,67,512.50 or, 1,75,67,513-.

   Interest on INR amount @9.35% pa for 85 days = (1,75,67,513 x 85 x 9.35) / 36500

   = INR 382,515.

   Hence, amount to be credited to current account of the exporter = INR (1,75,67,513 – 3,82,515) = INR 1,71,84,998.

7. This is a case of calculating TT Selling rate for USD.

   TT Selling rate = 91.5700 + 0.25% = 91.5700 + 0.2289 = 91.7989, or 91.80

8. This is a case of calculating the Bill Selling rate for CHF, after arriving at the CHF INR cross selling rate.

   CHF INR selling rate = 91.2250 / 0.7912 = 115.2995

   TT selling rate for CHF = 115.2995 + 0.20% = 115.2995 + 0.2306 = 115.5301

   Bill selling rate for CHF = 115.5301 + .40% = 115.5301 + 0.4621 = 115.9922, or 116.00.

EXERCISE 14

1. Since, this is a 60 days sight bill, the total time period involved for payment, including NTP of 25 days, is 85 days (25 + 60).

   Hence, this is a case of calculating EUR INR 85 days forward buying rate. Since the transaction is receipt of export proceeds and the forward rates of, both, USD INR and EUR USD pairs, are at premium, the bank will pass on only premium for 2 (not 3) months.

   Accordingly,

   USD INR 2 months forward buying rate = (90.3650 + 0.21) = 90.5750, and

   EUR USD 2 months forward buying rate = (1.1624 + (32.96/10000) = 1.1624 + 0.0033)

   = 1.1657

   ∴EUR INR 2 months forward interbank buying rate = 90.5750 x 1.1657 = 105.5833, and,

   EUR INR 2 months forward merchant buying rate = 105.5833 – 0.10%

   = 105.5833 – 0.1056

   = 105.4777, or **105.47**

2. Since this is a 30 days sight bill, the total time period involved for payment, including NTP of 25 days, is 55 days.

   Hence, this is a case of calculating HKD INR 55 days forward buying rate.

   It should be noted that whereas USD is quoted at a premium to INR, USD is quoted at a discount to HKD.

Accordingly, while calculating the HKD INR cross rate, the bank will pass on 1 month premium on the USD INR leg, but levy entire 2 months discount on the USD HKD leg.

USD INR 1 month forward buying rate = 90.3650 + 0.12 = 90.4850

USD HKD 2 month forward selling rate = 7.7980 – 0.02674 = 7.7713

Hence, HKD INR forward buying rate = 90.4850 ÷ 7.7713 = 11.6435

And, HKD INR bill buying rate = 11.6435 – 0.15% = 11.6435 – 0.0175

= 11.6260, or **11.62**

3. This is a case of calculation of AUD INR forward selling rate for delivery in May 2026.

   USD INR Spot / May selling rate = 92.2050 + 0.3500 = 92.5550

   AUD USD Spot / May selling rate = 0.7015 – 0.000927 = 0.700573, or 0.7006

   Hence, AUD INR May interbank selling rate = 92.5550 x 0.7006 = 64.8440

   And, AUD INR May forward merchant selling rate = 64.8440 + 0.20%

   = 64.8440 + 0.1297 = 64.9737, or **64.98**

4. This is a case of calculation of GBP INR bill selling rate for delivery June 2026.

   USD INR Spot / June = 92.1250 + 0.4100 = 92.5350

   GBP USD Spot / June = 1.3535 – 0.000684 = 1.352816, or 1.3528

   Hence, GBP INR Spot / June interbank rate = 92.5350 x 1.3528 = 125.1813

   And, GBP INR merchant Spot / June merchant selling rate = 125.1813 + 0.20% = 125.1813 + 0.2504 = 125.4317,

   And, GBP INR merchant Spot / June bill selling rate = 125.4317 + 0.35%

   = 125.4317 + 0.4390 = 125.8707, or **125.88**

EXERCISE 16

1. **WORKING**

   Using Rule 16.2 to solve the exercise.

   On 18/12/2025

   Merchant forward sale contract rate

   = 90.2725 + 0.64 = 90.9125 + 0.20% = 90.9125 + 0.1818 = 91.0943, or **91.10**

   On 16/1/2026

   IB forward buying rate

   = 90.5175 + 0.49 = **91.0075**

   IB spot selling rate

   = **90.5200**

a. Swap charges = Amount x (interbank forward buying rate - interbank spot selling rate on date of early delivery)

= 25,000 x (91.0075 – 90.5200) = 25000 x 0.4875 = **INR 12,188 (+)**

b. Interest of funds flow = {(Amount x Forward selling contract rate given to customer) – (Amount x interbank spot selling rate on date of early delivery)}

= 25000 x (91.10 – 90.5200) = 25000 x 0.5800 = + 14,500 **(net inflow)**

No. of days = 104 (ie., from 16/1/2026 to 30/4/2026)

Interest = (14500 x 104 x 4) ÷ 36500 = **INR 165**

Total charges for early delivery = 12,188 + 165 = INR 12,353- payable **to** importer.

2. WORKING

Using Rule 16.1 to solve the exercise.

On 18/12/2025

Merchant forward purchase rate = (90.2700 + 0.52) - 0.10% = 90.79 - 0.10% =

90.79 - 0.0908 = 90.6992, or **90.69**

On 16/1/2026

IB spot buying rate = **90.5175**

IB forward selling rate = 90.5200 + 0.51 = **91.0300**

a. Swap charges = Amount x (interbank spot buying rate – interbank forward selling rate on date of early delivery)

= 25,000 x (90.5175 – 91.0300) = 25,000 x (-) 0.5125 = (-) **12,813**

b. Interest on funds = {(Amount x interbank spot buying rate on date of early delivery) - (Amount x Forward purchase contract rate given to customer)}

= 25000 x (90.5175 - 90.69) = 25000 x (-) 0.1725 = INR (-) 4313 **(net outflow for Bank)**

No. of days = 104

Interest = (-4313 x 104 x 8) ÷ 36500 = (-) **INR 98.**

Total charges for early delivery = (-) INR (12813 + 98) = (-) INR 12,911, ie., payable **by** the exporter.

3. **WORKING**

Using Rule 16.1 to solve the exercise.

On 8/10/2025

Merchant forward purchase rate = (103.9544 – 0.15%) = 103.9544 – 0.1559

= 103.7985 or, **103.79**

On 4/11/2025

IB spot buying rate = **103.2552**

IB forward selling rate = **104.0582**

a. Swap charges = Amount x (interbank spot buying rate – interbank forward selling rate on date of early delivery)

= 35500 x (103.2552 – 104.0582) = 35500 x (-) 0.8030 = **(-) 28,507**

b. Interest on funds = {(Amount x interbank spot buying rate on date of early delivery) - (Amount x Forward purchase contract rate given to customer) }

= 35500 x (103.2552 - 103.79) = 35500 x (-) 0.5348 = INR (-) 18,985 **(net outflow for Bank)**

No. of days = 57 (ie., from 4/11/2025 to 31/12/2025)

Interest = (- 18985 x 57 x 8) ÷ 36500 = (-) **INR 237.**

Total charges for early delivery = (-) INR (28507 + 237) = (-) INR 28,744, ie., payable **by** the exporter.

4. **WORKING**

Using Rule 16.2 to solve the exercise. Moreover, cross rates of HKD INR have to be worked out for spot and forward.

On 8/1/2026

Calculation of Merchant HKD INR forward sale contract rate

USD INR forward sale rate = (89.8700 + 0.74) = 90.6100

USD HKD forward buying rate = 7.7860 – (464.85/10000) = 7.7860 – 0.0465

= 7.7395 (USD is at discount to HKD)

HKD INR forward selling rate = 90.61 ÷ 7.7395 = 11.7075

HKD INR merchant forward selling rate = 11.7075 + 0.25% = 11.7075 + 0.0293

= 11.7368. or **11.74**

On 11/3/2026

Calculation of IB HKD INR forward buying rate

USD INR forward buying rate = 92.23 + 0.47 = 92.7000

USD HKD forward selling = 7.8241 - (209.78 / 10000) = 7.8241 – 0.0210

= 7.8031

HKD INR forward buying rate = 92.7000 / 7.8031 = **11.8799**

IB HKD INR spot selling rate

= 92.2325 / 7.8237 = **11.7889**

a. Swap charges = Amount x (interbank forward buying rate - interbank spot selling rate on date of early delivery)

= 45,000 x (11.8799 – 11.7889) = 45000 x 0.0910 = **(+) INR 4,095**

b. Interest of funds flow = {(Amount x Forward selling contract rate given to customer) – (Amount x interbank spot selling rate on date of early delivery)}

= 45000 x (11.74 – 11.7889) = 45000 x (-) 0.0489 = (-) 2,201 **(net outflow)**

No. of days = 81 (ie., from 11/3/2026 to 31/5/2026)

Interest = (- 2201 x 81 x 8) ÷ 36500 = (-) **INR 39**

Total charges for early delivery = 4,095 - 39 = INR 4,056 payable **to** importer.

EXERCISE 17

1. This is a case of booking of EUR INR forward purchase contract and cancellation of the same, prior to due date.

WORKING

On 4/2/2026 - EUR INR Forward Purchase contract booking

USD INR forward rate = 90.4250 + 0.22 = 90.6450

EUR USD forward rate = 1.1334 + (17.29/10000) = 1.1334 + 0.0017 = 1.1351

EUR INR forward rate = 90.6450 x 1.1351 = 102.8911

EUR INR merchant forward purchase rate = 102.8911 – 0.20% = 102.8911 – 0.2058

= 102.6853, or **102.68**

On 14/3/2026 – EUR INR forward selling rate

USD INR forward rate = 92.5825 + 0.43 = 93.0125

EUR USD forward rate = 1.1516 + (21.90 / 10000) = 1.1516 + 0.0022 = 1.1538

EUR INR forward rate = 93.0125 x 1.1538 = 107.3178

EUR INR merchant forward selling rate = 107.3178 + 0.25% = 107.3178 + 0.2683

= 107.5861, or **107.59**

Calculation of cancellation charges

Charges = 75,000 x (102.68 – 107.59) = 75000 x (-) 4.91 = INR 368,250 **to be paid by the exporter.**

2. This is a case of booking of CAD INR forward sale contract and cancellation of the same, prior to due date.

   WORKING

   On 15/12/2025 - CAD INR Forward sale contract booking

   USD INR forward sale contract rate = 90.6575 + 0.61 = 91.2675

   USD CAD forward purchase rate = 1.3770 – (71.05÷10000) = 1.3770 – 0.0071

   = 1.3699

   CAD INR forward rate = 91.2675 / 1.3699 = 66.6235

   CAD INR merchant forward selling rate = 66.6235 + 0.25% = 66.6235 + 0.1666

   = 66.7901, or **66.80**

   On 3/3/2026 - CAD INR Forward purchase contract booking

USD INR forward purchase rate = 91.5625 + 0.41 = 91.9725

USD CAD forward sale rate = 1.4502 – (21.35 ÷10000) = 1.4502 – 0.0021

= 1.4481

CAD INR rate = 91.9725 ÷ 1.4481 = 63.5125

CAD INR merchant forward purchase rate = 63.5125 – 0.20% = 63.5125 – 0.1270

= 63.3855, or **63.38**

Charges = 22,000 x (63.38 – 66.80) = 22000 x (-) 3.42 = INR 75,240 **to be paid by the importer.**

3. This is a case of booking of USD INR forward sale contract and cancellation of the same, on due date.

   WORKING

   On 15/12/2025 - USD INR Forward sale contract booking

   USD INR forward sale rate = (90.6575 + 0.39) + 0.20% = 91.0475 + 0.20% =

   91.0475 + 0.1821 = 91.2296, or **91.23**

   On 28/2/2026 – USD INR TT buying rate

   USD INR TT buying rate = 91.0800 – 0.10% = 91.0800 – 0.0911

   = 90.9889, or **90.98**

   Charges = 18,000 x (90.98 – 91.23) = 18000 x (-) 0.25 = INR 4,500 **to be paid by the company.**

4. This is a case of booking of AUD INR forward purchase contract and cancellation of the same, on due date.

   WORKING

   On 15/12/2025 - AUD INR merchant forward purchase contract booking

   USD INR forward buying rate = (90.6550 + 0.28) = 90.9350

   AUD USD forward buying rate = 0.6955 – (2.6÷10000) = 0.6955 – 0.0003 = 0.6952

   AUD INR forward buying rate = 90.9350 x 0.6952 = 63.2180

   AUD INR merchant forward buying rate = 63.2180 – 0.15% = 63.2180 – 0.0948

   = 63.1232, or **63.12**

   On 28/2/2026 – AUD INR TT selling rate

   USD INR spot selling rate = 90.6575

   AUD USD spot selling rate = 0.7120

   AUD INR spot selling rate = 90.6575 x 0.7120 = 64.5481

   AUD INR TT selling rate = 64.5481 – 0.25% = 64.5481 – 0.1614

   = 64.3867, or **64.39**

   Charges = 52,000 x (63.12 – 64.39) = 52000 x (-) 1.27 = INR 66,040 **to be paid by the exporter.**

EXERCISE 18

1. This is a case of booking of USD INR forward sale contract and extension of the same on its due date.

   WORKING

   On 1/1/2026

   USD INR merchant forward sale contract rate = 90.0225 + 0.28 = 90.3025 + 0.15%

   = 90.3025 + 0.1355 = 90.4380, or 90.44

   On 27/2/2026

   USD INR TT buying rate = 91.1050 – 0.10% = 91.1050 – 0.0911 = 91.0139, or 91.01

   Extension charges = 25,000 x (91.01 – 90.44) = 25,000 x 0.57 = **14,250 payable to the importer.**

   Fresh forward sale contract rate, delivery April 2026 = (91.1075 + 0.32) + 0.15%

   = 91.4275 + 0.1371 = 91.5646, or **91.57**.

2. This is a case of booking of USD INR forward purchase contract and extension of the same on due date.

   WORKING

   On 21/11/2025

   USD INR merchant forward purchase contract rate = 89.6275 + 0.35 = 89.9775 - 0.10%

   = 89.9775 - 0.0900 = 89.8875, or 89.88

   On 31/1/2026

   USD INR TT selling rate = 91.6850 + 0.15% = 91.6850 + 0.1375 = 91.8225, or 91.83

Extension charges = 35,000 x (89.88 – 91.83) = 35,000 x (-) 1.95 = **68,250 payable by the exporter.**

Fresh forward purchase contract rate, delivery March 2026 = (91.6825 + 0.26) - 0.10%

= 91.9425 - 0.0919 = 91.8506, or **91.85**.

3. This is a case of booking of USD INR forward sale contract and extension of the same prior to its due date.

   WORKING

   On 25/11/2025

   USD INR merchant forward sale contract rate = 92.26

   On 15/12/2025

   USD INR merchant forward buying rate, delivery February 2026 = 90.7700 + 0.35

   = 91.1200 – 0.10% = 91.1200 – 0.0911 = 91.0289, or 91.02.

   Extension charges = 45,000 x (91.02 – 92.26) = 45,000 x (-) 1.24 = **55,800 payable by the customer.**

   Fresh forward sale contract rate, delivery Feb 2026 = (90.7725 + 0.52) + 0.20%

   = 91.2925 + 0.1826 = 91.4751, or **91.48**.

4. This is a case of booking of USD INR forward purchase contract and extension of the same, prior to its due date.

   WORKING

   On 4/11/2025

   USD INR merchant forward purchase contract rate = 88.80

   On 4/12/2025

USD INR TT forward sale rate, delivery December, 2025 = 90.1550 + 0.21 = 90.3650

= 90.3650 + 0.25% = 90.3650 + 0.2259 = 90.5909, or 90.60

Extension charges = 100,000 x (88.80 – 90.60) = 100,000 x (-) 1.80 = **1,80,000 payable by the exporter.**

Fresh forward purchase contract rate, delivery Feb 2026 = (90.1525 + 0.34) - 0.15%

= 90.4925 - 0.1357 = 90.3568, or **90.35**.

Glossary

A

Arbitrage – Buying and selling of currency in different markets to earn profit on a riskless basis.

Ask Rate – Selling rate.

B

Balance of Payments – The net position of all international payments and receipts of a country.

Base Currency – The currency that appears on the left-hand side of a currency quote.

Bid Rate – Buying rate.

C

Cash Transaction – A transaction with value date same as transaction date.

Chain Rule – The process by which exchange rate for a currency is derived through the exchange rate of an intermediate currency.

Cover Operation – A transaction by which a bank buys or sells against its merchant transaction in the interbank market.

Cross Rate – The exchange rate for a currency derived through the exchange rate of an intermediate currency.

D

Deep Market – Market with a large number of transactions.

Direct Quotation – A quote where price of one unit of foreign currency is stated in terms of domestic currency.

Discount – A forward margin that makes a currency cheaper in the future.

E

Exchange Margin – Profit margin retained by banks while quoting merchant rates.

F

Foreign Currency – Currency of a country other than the home country.

Foreign Exchange – Conversion of one currency into another.

Forward Contract – An agreement where a bank agrees today to quote an exchange rate for a foreign currency for a future date.

Forward Margin – Difference between spot rate and forward rate.

Forward Transaction – A transaction with value date greater than two business days after transaction date.

H

Hedging – Strategy used to protect from currency fluctuations.

Home Currency – Currency of the home country.

I

Indirect Quotation – A quote where price of one unit of domestic currency is stated in terms of foreign currency.

Interbank Market – Market where banks deal with each other.

Interbank Rate – Forex rate quoted by one bank to another bank.

Interbank Transaction – Transaction between two banks.

L

Loro Account – Your account with them.

M

Market – A place where buyers and sellers come together to buy or sell goods and services.

Market Maker – A bank which quotes both buying and selling rates simultaneously.

Market Taker – A bank which quotes only buying or selling rate.

Merchant Rate – Forex rate quoted by a bank to its customer.

Merchant Transaction – Transaction between a bank and its customer.

N

Nostro Account – Our account with you.

O

Offer Rate – Selling rate.

Over Bought – Situation where a bank has bought more foreign currency than it has sold.

Over Sold – Situation where a bank has sold more foreign currency than it has bought.

P

Pip – In most traded currencies, the 4th decimal place; in some currencies like JPY, the 2nd decimal place.

Pipette – The 5th decimal place used in highly traded currencies.

Premium – A forward margin that makes a currency more expensive in the future.

Q

Quoted Currency – The currency that appears on the right-hand side of a currency quote.

S

Shallow Market – Market with few transactions.

Speculation – Taking a view on a market without complete information.

Spot Transaction – Transaction with value date equal to transaction date + two business days.

Spread – Difference between buying and selling rates.

Swap – Simultaneous buying and selling of a foreign currency.

Swap Cost – Cost incurred while undertaking a swap transaction.

Swap Points – Difference between spot rate and forward rate.

T

Tom Transaction – Transaction with value date equal to transaction date + one business day.

Two-Way Quote – A quote containing both buying and selling rates.

V

Volatility – Frequency and magnitude of rapid price changes in a currency pair.

Vostro Account – Your account with us.

www.ingramcontent.com/pod-product-compliance
Lightning Source LLC
LaVergne TN
LVHW052303200926
848481LV00002B/453